Assessing IT Projects to Ensure Successful Outcomes

Assessing IT Projects to Ensure Successful Outcomes

KERRY R. WILLS

it gp™

IT Governance Publishing

IT Governance Publishing
IT Governance Limited
Unit 3, Clive Court
Bartholomew's Walk
Cambridgeshire Business Park
Ely
Cambridgeshire
CB7 4EA
United Kingdom

www.itgovernance.co.uk

First published in the United Kingdom in 2015
by IT Governance Publishing
ISBN 978-1-84928-736-4

PREFACE

For two decades I have managed several large information technology (IT) programs totaling more than one billion US dollars in size, as well as assessed and remediated several troubled programs. Therefore, I have both received and conducted many project assessments and also have a deep empirical background in how to run technology projects and programs. Based on this experience, I decided to write this book on project assessments, taken from the perspective of a practitioner of project management.

I believe that successful information technology project delivery is a result of a well-organized project structure and the execution of the project using strong project management processes. Therefore, this book will focus mainly on the areas of project structure and project management, and less on the software delivery lifecycle (SDLC) process.

The intention is not for this book to be a formal model on how to perform IT audits, as there are plenty of industry standard materials and organizations that do this well. Rather, the intention is to focus on the content of the assessment which includes the main functions of project management and delivery (e.g. schedule management, resource management and program structure), and how to assess that they are structured and being used properly to ensure successful project outcomes.

This book is organized as a reference guide for assessing the key project management functions within a project. It also uses real world project management experience to identify important concepts to consider, themes to look for, checklists which can be leveraged, and case studies from real assessments to demonstrate the main points.

On the cover of this book is a picture of a compass which I think is an appropriate metaphor for how this book is written and intended. The focus should not be on the markings on the compass, or how shiny it may be, but on how it is used and the direction in which it is pointing, to enable the user of it to meet their destination. Similarly, a project assessment is not about checking boxes and having the best framework for auditing but rather ensuring that the use of the assessment optimizes value, and ultimately enables the projects to be successful (and thus the title of this book).

ACKNOWLEDGEMENTS

It is important to recognize those people who helped and supported me to write this book which is my third on project management.

- My wife, Diane, for supporting me during the many hours of being locked away in my study writing this book.
- My children, Stephanie and Matthew, who inspire me every day to be the best that I can be.
- My parents, for instilling in me the values to think differently, trust my instincts, and to follow my dreams.
- The many team members on projects I have worked who taught me the lessons that are collected in this book.
- Matthew Conboy for reviewing the concept and providing his insights and experience.
- Brian Johnson, Chris Evans, ITSM Specialist, and Dan Swanson, Dan Swanson and Associates for their helpful comments during the review process.
- IT Governance Publishing for providing guidance and support through the publishing process.

ABOUT THE AUTHOR

Kerry Wills has worked as a Consultant and a Project Manager for Fortune 500 corporations on multi-million dollar technology projects since 1995. During that time he has gained experience in several capacities; as a program manager, project manager, architect, developer, business analyst and tester. Having worked in each of these areas gives Kerry a deep understanding of all facets of an information technology project. Kerry has planned and executed several large programs, as well as assessed and remediated several troubled programs.

Kerry is a member of Mensa and has a unique perspective on project work, resulting in 11 patents, published work in project management journals and books, and speaking engagements at dozens of project management conferences and corporations around the world. Kerry has written two prior books focused on the evolving skills of project managers (*Essential Project Management Skills* in 2010) and on running programs using a consultative approach (*Applying Guiding Principles of Effective Program Delivery* in 2013).

x

CONTENTS

CHAPTER 1: CONTEXT

Increasingly, corporations are investing more money into information technology (IT) solutions and projects. Forrester Research estimated that worldwide spending on information technology in 2013 topped two trillion US dollars (Forrester 2013). A significant amount of this spend will come in the form of IT projects and programs. The Standish Group estimates that we spend more than $250 billion each year on IT application development of around 175,000 projects (Standish, 2014).

In addition to the increased spend on technology, there are several other trends in the marketplace which should be recognized. *Figure 1.1* highlights some of these trends with their associated impacts on technology projects.

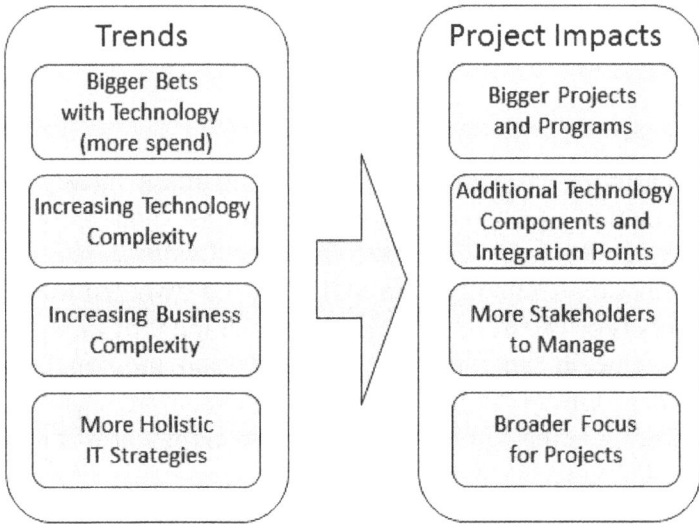

Figure 1.1: Business and technology trends impacting projects

Market trends

- Corporations are placing larger bets on technology investments and strategies, meaning they are spending significant amounts of money on technology solutions, products and projects. Even one decade ago, a program costing 25 million US dollars was considered "big", and now it is not uncommon for a corporation to be managing multiple programs that cost more than nine figures in US dollars, and that span more than three years in duration. Technology can be used as a strategic advantage for corporations, and so technology projects are getting more funding than ever before, for corporations to remain competitive in the marketplace.

- Technology is increasingly becoming more and more complicated with multiple tiered architectures, complex infrastructure designs, many different integration points between applications, and thousands of customized and packaged solutions being introduced into the marketplace.

- Business trends also continue to evolve to more complicated organizations, processes and operating models. One example includes corporations becoming more specialized and tailored to customer's interests which means more deviations of business products which need to be configured to meet differing customer expectations.

- As corporations increase their spend on technology, they are also introducing larger and more holistic technology strategies, such as standardizing on specific technology assets, or looking for ways to rationalize large portfolios of technologies, infrastructure, applications and software products. There is also the increase in cyber attacks and security threats, requiring ever more complex and expensive security packages.

As these market trends evolve, they have implications on corporations and how they invest their money and manage their operations. These implications also then influence how technology projects get identified, managed and tracked.

Impact of trends

- Corporations making larger bets with technology results in an increasing size of programs, projects and workstreams. This now requires multiple project managers and resources to work across the different projects (such as end-to-end requirements, solution or testing leads). These projects also have interdependencies with each other which need to be planned out and managed.

- Increasing complexity of technology means there are now more applications, interfaces and products involved in the technology solutions. This additional complexity results in more technology components and assets that have to be planned for, designed, built, integrated and tested. Also, the increasing risk of cyber attacks means additional security technology is required in the solutions.
- Increasing business and organizational complexity results in more project stakeholders which need to be understood, managed and communicated to. It is not uncommon today for a project to have many stakeholders, from different organizations, that have different agendas and expectations.
- Broader technology strategies also impact projects by introducing additional considerations, such as designing solutions which may have to consider requirements beyond just the project. Another example is using enterprise standard technology solutions, which may not exactly meet the business requirements but are mandated.

Because of these trends and associated impacts, it is clear that projects are becoming larger, more complex, and more difficult to manage. As a result of this increasing complexity, project success rates remain very low. The Standish Group publishes a report of project success and failure every year based on comprehensive analysis, and the following metrics demonstrate the challenges (Standish 2014):

- 31% of projects will be cancelled before they get completed.
- 52.7% of projects will cost nearly double (189%) of their original financial estimates.

- Only 16% of projects get completed on time and on budget; with a rate of 9% for large corporations.
- Completed projects deliver on approximately 42% of the originally planned scope and features.

There are consequences to these project failures which can go beyond delayed schedules, incomplete scope and additional cost. Some of the impacts can include the following:

- A delayed capability which would enable a corporation to enter a new market, deploy a new business product, or have a competitive advantage in their industry.

- A delay to critical infrastructure which could impact corporation operations and possibly security as well.

- An impact to a customer-facing capability which would, in turn, result in an impact to customer satisfaction, loyalty and brand reputation.

- Possible compliance risks and penalties associated with missing key government mandated milestones.

- Any of the above items could impact the corporation reputation in the marketplace, as well as the stock price and stockholder confidence.

With corporations investing more money into technology projects and success remaining low, with significant implications, it is critical to ensure that the projects meet their objectives and commitments. One way of doing this is to perform an assessment, or audit, of projects at key points during their schedule, to look for trends, gaps or challenges, and to take some action to minimize, or mitigate, the risks.

This book was written with the intent of identifying and structuring how to perform an IT project assessment, along with some important concepts to consider. The book is organized into five main sections:

1. *Approach* – this first section will identify the types of assessment that can be conducted, and then outline the approach for conducting an assessment, with the key steps in the process. This section will also identify the differences between a project and program assessment, as well as key considerations based on the experiences of the author, having conducted and received many project assessments.

2. *Plan* – this section reviews the activities and considerations required to plan for the assessment, including determining which approach to take, developing the assessment plan, preparing the inventories of questions and documents, and planning for any logistics required to conduct the assessment.

3. *Collect information* – the third section details out how to collect key project information from interviews and document reviews. The information is organized into several functional areas of managing projects including finance management, scope management and schedule management. Each function will be described, along with key questions to ask during the interviews, and documents to look for. There will also be considerations, and a case study for each area, to provide a real world context.

4. *Assess and recommend* – this fourth section focuses on what to do once the relevant project information is gathered and gets assessed. This includes looking for consistent themes, key considerations to be aware of,

identifying challenges and gaps, and then providing a set of practical recommendations to mitigate, or address, the risks, challenges and themes which have been identified.

5. *Package and present* – the last section of the book highlights the best ways to package the assessment for different stakeholders, and then present the findings in a way that conveys the key messages of the assessment. It also provides some examples of how to package the findings, based on different audiences or stakeholders.

The book also contains a summary section which highlights the key points from the book, as well as providing some checklists which can be used in conducting assessments. These include a list of common IT roles, interview questions by role, and key focus areas for project document reviews.

The targeted audience for this book is professionals who are assessing projects, such as internal auditors, framework auditors, project assessors or external consultants. This book can also be used for project managers looking for a comprehensive view of key artifacts and an approach for managing projects, or as a means of preparing for an assessment of their project. This information can be used to assess projects reactively but can also be used proactively, as a checklist of considerations and activities to plan, and manage, a project. Note that this book assumes that there is proficiency in project management principles of the person/team performing the assessment, and therefore does not go into details for each project management topic.

CHAPTER 2: ASSESSMENT APPROACH

In order to optimize the process and maximize the outcomes of a project assessment, it is important to take a methodical and deliberate approach to the review. This chapter will identify several types of project assessments, and then detail out the key steps performed during an assessment. The chapter will also distinguish between project and program assessments, and provide some insights around key lessons to consider when determining the project assessment approach.

2.1 Types of assessments

There are several types of information technology project assessments which can be conducted. *Table 2.1* identifies and describes the most common types of project audits or assessment with their associated focus areas, and identification of what type of resource is typically conducting the assessment.

Table 2.1: Assessment types and their characteristics

Type	Description	Focus	Assessor
Project Audit	Larger initiatives with high cost or significant benefits being assessed for risk. May be part of a corporation risk management	Focused on delivery risks, adherence to corporation standards and controls.	Generally performed by an internal audit organization within the corporation where the project is being

	approach.		delivered.
Software Delivery Lifecycle (SDLC) Assessment or Phase Gate	In some SDLC frameworks there are audits, or gates, where a project needs to confirm compliance before moving on to the next phase. Can also be done at the end of the project for lessons learned.	Adherence to software delivery lifecycle standards, or completion of one phase before moving to the next.	Generally performed by internal SDLC framework team.
Troubled Project Assessment	Requested by senior management to assess projects which have significant risks and issues.	Understanding risk and problem areas, with the intention of providing recommendations to remediate.	Generally performed by external resources (e.g. consultants) that have large project experience.
Post Implementation Review	Facilitate and document lessons learned after a project has been completed.	Lessons learned and best practices which can be used to augment future projects and the corporation frameworks.	Generally performed by the standard framework team.
Readiness Assessment	Review high level requirements and plan to determine if the project should be funded.	Scope, cost and schedule for an initiative.	Could be performed by audit, consultants, or a portfolio review team.

While there are different types of assessments, the approach for each of these types of project assessment is roughly the same. The content of the themes and recommendations, as well as the packaging, may be different, however, since these types each have slightly different objectives and audiences. Note that the word "assessment" will be used going forward in the book as a general representation of all of these types, and where there are differences they will be called out.

2.2 Approach

At the highest level, conducting a technology assessment requires four basic steps which are outlined in *Figure 2.1*. The assessment needs to be planned out, followed by a period of collecting key project information from various sources. Following this, the assessment team analyzes the information and determines some recommendations. Finally, the assessment is packaged, and presented, to key stakeholders.

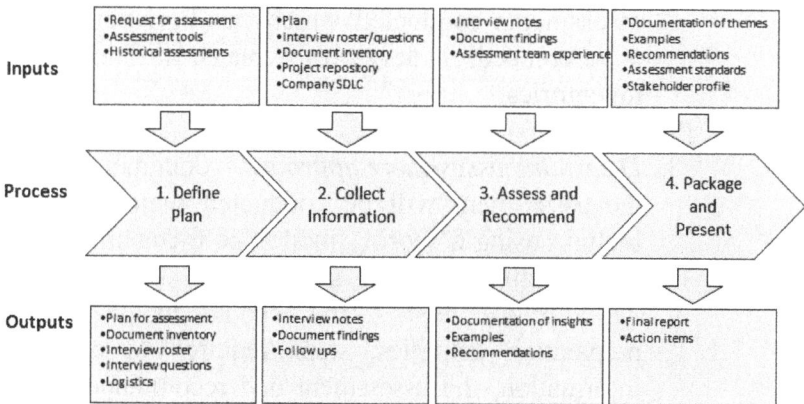

Inputs	•Request for assessment •Assessment tools •Historical assessments	•Plan •Interview roster/questions •Document inventory •Project repository •Company SDLC	•Interview notes •Document findings •Assessment team experience	•Documentation of themes •Examples •Recommendations •Assessment standards •Stakeholder profile
Process	1. Define Plan	2. Collect Information	3. Assess and Recommend	4. Package and Present
Outputs	•Plan for assessment •Document inventory •Interview roster •Interview questions •Logistics	•Interview notes •Document findings •Follow ups	•Documentation of insights •Examples •Recommendations	•Final report •Action items

Figure 2.1: Typical assessment approach

1. *Define plan* – the first step in the assessment process is to determine the plan for the review. This is the pre-work before the assessment starts, and includes the planning around the approach to take, which team members to interview, what questions to ask during the interviews, what project documents to review, and any logistics required to perform the assessment.
   a. Inputs
      i. *Request for assessment* – usually an assessment is requested by a project stakeholder that has a specific set of objectives for the assessment (e.g. identify risks, confirm controls, etc.), or this could be a planned review as part of a standard delivery phase gate framework, or a corporation audit schedule.
      ii. *Assessment tools* – collection of any standard processes, templates, checklists or documents which will be used when conducting the assessment.
      iii. *Historical assessments* – any similar project assessments conducted which can be leveraged, or referenced, to develop the plans, questions or inventories.
   b. Process
      i. *Determine assessment approach* – document how the assessment will be conducted which could include using a scoring model, or focusing more on qualitative risks and gaps.
      ii. *Develop the plan* – this should include any preparation activities, steps required to collect information, the assessment and recommendation activities, as well as activities to prepare, and deliver, the report. The plan should include activity durations, dependencies, start and stop dates, and

the names of the people assigned to the activities.

 iii. *Document the inventories* – the key to a successful assessment is in having the right information, so it is important to determine what information is needed. Inventories should be developed around what documents are needed, which people should be interviewed, and what questions to ask during the interviews.

 iv. *Plan for the assessment* – logistics need to be considered and accounted for, such as areas to conduct the interviews, access to documents, email protocols, communications to team members, and scheduling a kick off meeting.

c. Outputs

 i. *Plan for the project assessment* – this includes activities aligned to the determined assessment approach, with dates and resource names assigned to each.

 ii. *Inventory of documents to review* – identifies which types of documents and evidence are needed to meet assessment objectives. These could be grouped by project function (e.g. schedule management, resources and vendors).

 iii. *Roster of people to interview* – since project teams have different roles, the targeted roles and specific named resources should be documented (e.g. business analyst, tester and developer).

 iv. *Inventory of questions to ask* – different project roles will have specific focus and insights and therefore require targeted questions, so questions should be organized by role.

 v. Logistics including meeting locations, access to documents and communications.

2. *Collect information* – once the assessment begins, it is important to collect as much relevant information as possible to inform the analysis. There are two primary methods of collecting information; interviewing project team members and collecting project documents.
   a. Inputs
      i. *Assessment plan* – this will lay out the key steps and timelines to collect the information, with the associated team members performing the activities.
      ii. *Interview roster and questions* – collect information through interview questions tailored towards team members, and soliciting role-specific insight.
      iii. *Document inventory* – collect relevant information contained in project documents related to specific project functions and the objectives of the assessment.
      iv. *Project repository* – the primary source of documents maintained by the project team.
      v. *Corporation SDLC framework* – many corporations have standard frameworks that they use for application development. This will be valuable for understanding the delivery expectations of the corporation for activities, templates and roles.
   b. Process
      i. *Conduct interviews* – facilitating conversations with key project team members and stakeholders to gather insights, observations and perceptions regarding the project, and aligned to the objectives of the project assessment.
      ii. *Assess documents* – reviewing key project documents supporting various project functions.

c. Outputs
  i. *Interview notes* – key points, quotes and observations from the team member interviews.
  ii. *Document findings* – key findings, observations, and comments from the review of project documents.
  iii. *Follow ups* – as a result of interviews and document reviews, there will be action items which require attention. These should be used to iterate through this step of collecting information.
3. *Assess and recommend* – review the outcomes of the project information collection step, looking for trends, risks and areas of improvement. Then, determine practical recommendations and action items for improvement opportunities and the mitigations of risks.
  a. Inputs
    i. *Interview notes* – any key points, insights and perceptions identified by project team members.
    ii. *Document findings* – any relevant findings, facts, examples and evidence found in the project documents.
    iii. *Assessment team experience* – the assessment team should come with empirical backgrounds in project delivery and project assessments which can be used to determine recommendations based on their experience and history.
  b. Process
    i. *Assess inputs* – review the collected information and look for "themes" that span across project documents and interviews. It is also important to gather specific examples to support the themes which will be useful for packaging and presenting the assessment, and add to the credibility of the

review.

ii. *Identify gaps* – compare the discovered project information to corporation standards and the assessment objectives, to look for any gaps, challenges or risks.

iii. *Develop recommendations* – develop a set of actionable recommendations to remediate identified challenges, close gaps, and mitigate project delivery risks.

c. Outputs

i. *Documentation of themes, gaps and observations* – these are the aggregate insights and observations based on the assessment of information collected.

ii. *Examples* – specific points, facts, or project documents which support the findings.

iii. *Recommendations* – aligned to the identified gaps, risks and challenges, with the intention of improving the project delivery. These recommendations should be aligned to the objectives of the assessment.

4. *Package and present* – package the analysis, findings and recommendations, and then present them to key stakeholders.

a. Inputs

i. *Documentation of themes, gaps and observations* – the results of the information assessment.

ii. *Examples* – these could be documents, or facts, which substantiate the documented themes.

iii. *Recommendations* – any identified actions that the assessment team is proposing to address the noted risks and challenges.

iv. *Assessment standards* – any standard templates or processes required to package the assessment report.

v. *Stakeholder profile* – an identification of the key stakeholders to be presented to and their profiles, which could inform the way that the report gets created and presented.

b. Process

i. *Package the report* – organize the assessment into the report which includes the findings, themes and recommendations. It can also include the approach taken, and a list of people interviewed and documents reviewed, as appendix materials.

ii. *Communication plan* – definition of the plan to communicate findings and recommendations.

iii. *Present* – reviewing the report with key stakeholders and senior management.

c. Outputs

i. *Final report out* – including supporting materials, summary and details.

ii. *Action plan* – listing of key actions, with names and dates associated to them. Actions may include follow ups on the assessment, and future reviews of progress.

2.3 Project and programs

According to the Project Management Institute (PMI), *The Standard for Program Management* Third Edition (PMI 2013), "A Program is a group of related projects managed in a coordinated manner to obtain benefits and control NOT available from managing them individually."

Because programs are aggregations of projects, they tend to be larger, and more complex, than individual projects.

Therefore, while the assessment steps are the same, the assessment focus for projects and programs should be different. *Table 2.2* highlights some examples of the differences between projects and programs when it comes to an IT assessment. Note that this book will use the term "project" assessment but where there are significant differences with programs, they will be identified.

Table 2.2: Examples of different assessment focus for projects and programs

Category	Project Focus	Program Focus
Structure	Organization of team within the project	Interrelationships between projects and roles that span across projects (e.g. requirements, solution and testing) within the program
Schedule	Critical path within the project and external dependencies	Critical path within the projects, as well as dependencies across projects, within the program, and externally
Resources	Roles within the project	Roles within the projects, and roles that span across projects (e.g. program solution lead or program testing lead)
Finances	Cost for the project and its components	Cost for individual projects and components within the program, as well as program-level costs that span projects
Governance	Project governance approach	Governance across projects and at the program level
Software Delivery Lifecycle (SDLC)	Following the SDLC within the project	Follow the SDLC within projects but also the management of project domains across projects (e.g. requirements management or test planning across projects)
Technology	The specific solutions	Technology solutions which

Solution	within the scope of the project	may span multiple projects, or even be external to the program and dependent on other projects

2.4 Considerations

There are several considerations to contemplate when planning and conducting the project assessment. The following considerations are meant to stimulate thought regarding how to approach the work, and what to look out for during the planning and execution of the project assessment.

Be practical

Projects can build up a large repository of documentation, and therefore information can get very detailed, redundant and abundant. For these reasons, it is important to be practical with the assessment approach in terms of what project information to seek, gather and review. For example, some documents are more valuable than others, and the assessment should focus on identifying the highest impact documents. Project assessments should focus on the highest value documents and not try to dilute their focus on reviewing every existing document in the project file repository. This will also allow for the assessment team to be efficient with their time and attention.

Timing is important

Stakeholders can ask for a project assessment at any time. Sometimes they can be done at key points on a project, such as the end of the requirements phase or design phase.

These assessments are usually part of a standard corporation delivery framework which includes planned checkpoints, or "gates", where key project information is reviewed for compliance to standards, and to confirm the quality is acceptable.

There are dozens of industry research papers on the impact of finding quality errors and defects late in the delivery cycles. *Figure 2.2* shows research from IBM System Sciences Institute which demonstrates that defects have a relatively low cost to find and fix in design, and get more expensive during coding (implementation) and testing, and then become exponentially higher if they get identified once the system is in production. Therefore, project assessments should seek to identify these quality gaps as early as possible, to minimize the higher cost of them being found later.

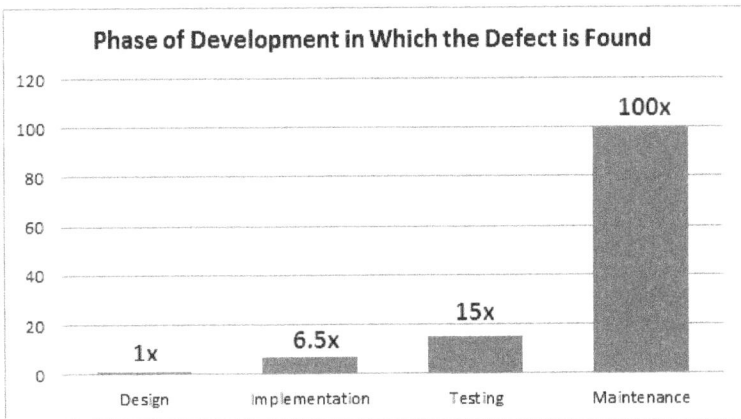

**Figure 2.2: Relative costs to fix software defects
(Source: IBM Systems Sciences Institute)**

Project assessments can also get requested when there is a sense from leaders that the project is in trouble (which usually means there is not a lot of lead time to take action and implement recommendations). The timing of the assessment is significant, as it will determine how much time the assessor has to review the project, what documents are available, and how quickly risks need to be addressed.

Promote safety

The terms "audit", or "assessment", can have negative connotations associated with them, related to the performance of the team or project manager, so it is important to communicate the objectives of the review. In most cases, the intent is not to "get" anyone but to identify risks, and opportunities, to improve the probability of success for the project. In fact, having team members "vent" is an important part to the assessment process because it identifies perceptions and frustrations from the project team members. Also, many assessments are conducted by external resources so that they are seen as a separate group that has objectivity, as opposed to an internal team which may have the appearance of a hidden agenda.

It may make sense to have a senior leader in the corporation announce the assessment and highlight these points. This will demonstrate leadership support of the assessment, introduce the assessment team, and proactively address any safety concerns that project team members may have.

Be efficient and cognizant of time

Assessments are usually conducted while the project is in-flight, so it is important for the assessment team to recognize this, and plan accordingly, with regards to the time of the project team members. The assessment should be planned out in such a way as to optimize the time of team members. For example, it may be better to review project documents and come prepared with specific questions prior to team member interviews, instead of having multiple iterations which can take additional time. Also consider bulking/chunking pieces of work, depending on the resource that will provide it, so you only hit them up once for the information, and maybe once more for follow up questions.

Manage expectations

There are several stakeholders in the assessment, and their expectations should be managed properly. This includes the sponsors of the assessment, the team members being assessed, and the project manager who is currently running the project. For the sponsors of the assessment, the team should determine the plan, with activities and the associated time (or cost), so that they can communicate the amount of work that is required and when the sponsors can receive the findings.

It is important to manage the expectations of the team members who are on the project being assessed. If the corporation follows a standard framework where the assessment is part of the process, then the team needs to agree, upfront, what deliverables will be expected and assessed. Another way of managing expectations is to communicate the plan and approach of the assessment, so the team is prepared for the interviews and compiles the appropriate project documentation.

It is just as important to manage the expectations of the stakeholders who are receiving the assessment report, so that they are clear as to what they will be receiving, and when they will be receiving it. The last thing that anyone wants is to spend time conducting an assessment that doesn't get the right attention from the project, or doesn't meet the goals and expectations of the stakeholders who asked for it.

Have credible assessors

It is essential for the assessors to be well versed in IT project delivery, and preferably have an empirical background in managing projects. This will allow them to recognize themes, and gaps, based on experience. It will also give them more credibility with the project team being assessed, so they are not viewed as someone reviewing their work that has less experience than the people who are being reviewed. It may also be good to have someone with experience outside of the corporation to bring in different methods or best practices.

The Institute for Internal Auditors confirms this important concept (IIA, 2009); "Even an auditor with a strong IT and business background may find many project management best practices unfamiliar." IIA suggests that internal auditors should take the time to learn project management processes and terminology.

If the assessment is looking at other specific domain areas, then experts in those areas should be considered for the assessment team. For example, if the assessment is looking at a specific technology solution, then the assessment team should have a technical expert on it. This could be a "guest auditor", who is someone that has extensive knowledge and is temporarily invited to help with the assessment. The assessment team needs to establish credibility so that the project team reveals pertinent information, and the stakeholders reviewing the report feel that it was developed by competent professionals.

Understand the culture

Corporations have their own cultures and subcultures which need to be understood and considered. For example, in some corporations the organizational hierarchy is very important and therefore the managers may want to see results before publishing them to more senior executives. Other corporation cultures may be more sensitive to how the report findings are worded, and may not like to see items in red because, at that corporation, red could mean people losing their jobs.

Individual projects may even have their own subcultures and politics between team members, or organizations working on the project, which need to be recognized before going too far into the assessment. For example, the project culture may be one where escalating any kind of risk is viewed poorly, and therefore the project documentation may not be revealing the true status and risks on the project, and show everything in "green" status. Recognizing this will help the assessment team to interpret the project information and, in turn, conduct a better project assessment.

Focus on facts

Team members can get very sensitive to being assessed and feel like they are personally being judged, and so it is important for the results to not look like they are blaming anyone. One of the ways to do this is to ensure that the assessment focuses on specific facts and examples with the work, and not with the individual team members. This takes away the debate on subjectivity, and highlights evidence instead of specific people. Facts are also important to demonstrate findings, justify key points, and call out the impact of a risk or recommended action. However, if there truly are challenges with specific resources, then those also need to have facts to identify the deficiencies.

Look for themes

There will be many findings during the project assessment, and it is important to recognize themes and trends in the information, as opposed to a focus on very unique and specific examples. There may be one example of one risk and, depending on the impact of that risk, it may not be a significant finding, or it may turn out to be a one-time activity. However, if there are multiple examples which demonstrate a recurring theme, then that would be important to recognize and document.

Consider complexity

Complexity is a significant contributor to risk, cost, and quality problems on technology projects. The assessment team should be on the lookout for complexity in processes, business products, technology solutions and organizational structure, and then seek to understand the implications of that complexity on the project. In many cases it may be a driver of risk and challenges on the project.

Trust but verify

A large amount of project information is collected during team member interviews including observations, identified risks, specific examples and perceived challenges. The assessment team should recognize that this could be considered anecdotal information, and seek to find project documents, evidence and facts which corroborate the comments and observations. This is especially important if multiple project team members bring up the same theme. This approach to gathering substantiating facts minimizes the possibility for debate over the findings when the assessment report gets packaged and communicated. It also takes away the focus from the team member who identified the specific item, and puts it on the facts that demonstrate the theme or observation.

Have consistent scoring

If the assessment approach is to "score" specific project or functional areas, then make sure that there is a consistent definition of the scores. For example, define what is a "low" score versus a "medium" or a "high" score. Not having consistent scoring can lead to confusion in the findings, as well as a loss of credibility for the assessment.

Be flexible with the plan

Just as projects go, many assessments do not follow the plans exactly as they are laid out initially, and so the assessment team should be flexible with their plans as scope and resources change, or as new insights are brought to bear. If there are significant changes which impact the objectives of the assessment, the team may want to consider communicating this to the sponsor of the assessment, to confirm, or modify, the approach.

Note that other considerations will be included throughout the book to supplement the key points, as appropriate.

CHAPTER 3: DEFINE THE PLAN

Planning is the critical first step in the assessment process. Having a solid plan for the assessment sets the pace for the assessment, and has many benefits which will ensure a successful assessment and maximize the value of the findings. Some of the benefits of proper planning are listed below:

- *Clarity of objectives* – the project assessment is being conducted based on a specific stakeholder request or set of goals and objectives. Therefore, it is important to document what these objectives are, and level-set the assessment approach based on meeting these objectives. For example, if the assessment is based on following corporation standards, then the focus may be on ensuring the right use of templates. Whereas an objective for successful delivery may look at the content within these deliverables, and how they are used to manage the project.

- *Begin with the end in mind* – by starting with determining the final package layout and structure, the assessment can be conducted in such a way as to facilitate the results in a manner which aligns to that structure. This is a much better approach than gathering a collection of information and then trying to figure out how to synthesize it into a cohesive report.

- *Focus on high value information* – the assessment lead, or team, should spend time, upfront, identifying what information, documents, or evidence will be gathered, as well as what team members to interview and what questions to ask them. Planning out what information to look for will enable the assessment to be focused on specific documents, and not having to sort through extraneous materials which will not contribute to the goals of the project review.

- *Be efficient with time* – with proper planning, the assessment can target key information, documents, and questions, which will then minimize the amount of iterations and follow up questions. Proper assessment planning will result in requiring significantly less time for the project team members involved in the assessment, as well as the people conducting the assessment.

- *Manage expectations for timing* – a detailed plan should include milestones, activities and durations. This can be used to manage the expectations of people being interviewed which should allow team members to plan accordingly for the time commitments. This can also help manage expectations for management, as to when to expect the report and recommendations.

- *Perception and credibility* – having a well thought out assessment plan conveys the perception that the team knows what they are doing, and that they have everything under control. Challenges, rework, and a perceived lack of structure on the assessment, will only cause the stakeholders to focus on the assessment team, and not the findings and recommendations of the review.

- *Tracking and reporting* – having a plan with the key activities allows the assessment team to track progress against that plan, and then report out to stakeholders on the status of the work.

- *"Eating your own dog food."* – it may seem hypocritical

for the assessment team to be reviewing the plans and structure of a project if they do not demonstrate those things in how the assessment is set up and conducted, which comes back to having credibility.

Before developing the plan it is essential to confirm the objectives and criteria of the assessment, so it may be helpful to develop a charter, or statement of work. This document should outline the objectives of the assessment, the team members who will be working on the assessment, the project areas being reviewed, the approach, the stakeholders requesting the assessment, and any expected outcomes. The plan should then be tailored around meeting these objectives and criteria.

3.1 Determine assessment approach

As part of the planning phase, the assessment team should determine how the assessment will be approached. By determining the approach upfront, this will allow the team to develop a plan, and organize the work in a way that will be easier to assess, and package, later in the process. There are several types of approaches which can be taken to gather, assess and report on the review findings.

Risk assessment

This type of assessment focuses on the identification of project delivery risks. This approach can be subjective, and focuses on the perceptions and observations of the team members being interviewed, as well as the assessors. Risks can also be gathered from reviewing project documents, such as risk logs and issues logs, but generally interviews are a more effective means of soliciting risks.

This is a good approach for using with troubled projects, or high risk projects, as it focuses on those areas which are the most significant to project delivery. It also looks at the impact of those risks, and makes suggestions to mitigate the risks and improve the chances of successful project delivery.

Gap assessment

This type of assessment starts with a list of expected activities or deliverables, and then compares the project to that list to identify gaps. In this case, the assessment team could start with a corporation framework checklist and determine if the project is using the appropriate documents and standards. This approach is most effective for a framework or SDLC assessment, to confirm that standards have been followed. For example, the team would look to confirm that the project has all the appropriate project management documentation, such as a plan, risk log, issue log and resource inventory, and that the proper SDLC templates are used for requirements, design and testing.

Scoring

A scoring assessment compares the project to a specific set of benchmarks. This is meant to be more quantitative. For example, a rating of "high", "medium", or "low" could be given to score the adherence to standards, or level of adequacy that a particular project function is being managed. Graphical representations, such as Harvey Balls, could also be used to highlight how well defined a particular project function is (e.g. partial shading for not well defined and full shading for well defined).

Resource competency

In some cases, the project leadership and sponsors may ask the assessment team to review the competency of key resources on the project. For example, they may want to assess how well the project manager is running the project, or how certain leads on the teams are performing in their roles. Project success is as much a function of the competency of the resources on the team, as it is a function of processes and methodologies used, so the assessment team should pay attention to resource capabilities.

Continuous improvement

Some assessments may be conducted after the project has completed, to look for best practices which can be applied to other projects, or the corporation standard framework. The review can also facilitate lessons learned from this project which can be applied back to future projects and other organizational processes.

Note that project assessments can use all of these methods for approaching the assessment but it is a good idea to think through these first. By determining how the information will be analyzed and packaged, the assessment team can tailor the plan, approach, interview questions and document gathering approach accordingly.

3.2 Develop the plan

Based on the assessment approach and objectives, the plan should be developed. The plan should include all of the activities required to complete the assessment, along with their associated duration, and the name of the person accountable for the activity. Activity dependencies should also be captured in the plan. For example, there are some activities which can be concurrent, such as collecting documents and interviewing team members. Some activities are sequential and dependent on each other, such as presenting the final report after the analysis has been made and the findings have been packaged.

In creating the plan, the assessor should leverage existing materials to identify and confirm the activities required. For example, historical assessments may provide a good starting point for developing the plan, since they will already have many of the key activities and lessons learned. Also, corporations sometimes have standards for conducting assessments which may include additional activities to consider and plan for, such as governance reviews. Lastly, it is important to contemplate and document any logistics required to conduct the project assessment in the plan.

It is important to list out all activities and specifics of the assessment so that they can be tracked and communicated. In large project assessments there may be dozens of documents to review and many team members to interview, so it is important to be able to see which activities are outstanding and not yet completed. This progress can then be reported on during regular meetings with the project stakeholders which should be documented and agreed to in the communication plan. Some stakeholders may also want early indications of findings, and the team should discuss these expectations so that it is clear what is being reported, when, and in what forum.

The following list is an example of a high level plan for conducting an IT project assessment, organized by the steps in the assessment process and including some of the key activities to perform.

- **Planning**
  o Create charter or statement of work
  o Collect historical information on similar assessments or benchmarks
  o Collect assessment tools and corporation standards for assessments
  o Confirm skills needed and assessment team
  o Determine location for assessment working files
  o Determine roles to be interviewed
  o Obtain list of names of people for each role requested
  o Create list of questions to ask, by role
  o Determine approach for capturing information from documents and team member interviews
  o Confirm logistics for interviews (e.g. phone, meeting room, etc.)
  o Obtain corporation frameworks and standards
  o Create list of documents and areas to focus on
  o Obtain access to project documents
  o Develop the plan of all activities to undertake in the assessment
  o Determine estimate of hours required to perform the assessment
  o Develop communications plan for stakeholders
  o Announce the assessment with applicable information, such as intent, timing and key activities
  o Schedule and conduct kick off to review the objectives, scope, timing and involvement for the assessment
- **Collect information**
  o Conduct team member interviews (list out each interview by name or role, so they can be tracked)

- o Collect and review project documents (list out by area and document, so they can be tracked)
- **Assess and recommend**
  - o Analyze findings from collected information
  - o Document themes, gaps and observations
  - o Conduct research necessary to score findings or assess the impact of the risks
  - o Determine recommendations
  - o Review findings
- **Package and present**
  - o Document high level findings or executive summary
  - o Document detailed findings with examples
  - o Document recommendations
  - o Package report with key project information and supplemental documentation, as appropriate
  - o Present results
  - o Schedule follow ups and next steps

3.3 Prepare the inventories

An important step in the planning process is to think through, and list out, the team members to interview, the questions to ask them, the inventory of project documents to review, and what to look for in those documents. Spending the time upfront preparing these inventories will ensure a smooth project assessment with minimal rework and follow ups, as well as attention on the most important parts of the project during the assessment. It is essential to ensure that the interviews and documents are focused on those areas which are identified in the objectives of the assessment. This will enable the assessment to meet its goals and be efficient with the time, resources, and materials being spent on it.

Planning for the interviews should start with the identification of which project roles will be reviewed, based on the stated objectives of the assessment and determined approach. *Table 7.1* (page 197) lists out and describes the typical roles on an IT project. Once the targeted project roles are identified to be interviewed, then specific team member names can be gathered for each of these roles. This becomes the inventory of project team members and roles to be interviewed. Next, the assessment team should determine what questions are to be asked of each team member and role. These questions should be specific, target the objectives, and seek to get examples whenever possible. There are several types of questions which could be asked during the assessment interviewing process:

- *General feeling* – ask about risks or overall view of the project, to leave the discussion open-ended for the interviewee. This could include asking for any recommendations or challenges that the person can identify. These questions allow the assessment team to understand the perceptions and morale of the team, as well as any risks which may not be captured in project documentation.

- *Role specific* – questions that relate to the project role of the team member being interviewed and their ability to perform their job including processes, tools and interactions with other team members and roles. For example, if the team is interviewing a business analyst, the questions could relate to the collection of business requirements and obtaining business sign offs.

- *Function specific* – questions that relate to one of the project management or software delivery lifecycle functions that are being assessed which could include processes, tools, role interactions or best practices. For example, asking specific questions related to the schedule management, resource management, or vendor management practices on the project.

- *Document specific* – as project documents get reviewed, questions or clarifications may arise which could be asked during the appropriate interview. For example, the team could ask the project manager questions about the current status report, or numbers from a financial worksheet.

An inventory of documents should also be developed to identify which project documents will be asked for, gathered and reviewed during the assessment. This document inventory can also be used as a means to track which files have been received, which documents are still outstanding, and the status of the document in the assessment process. *Tables 7.14* through *7.22* (pages 209–215) provide a sample of documents for each project functional area which should be considered for the document inventory, as well as some key areas to review for each. It may be helpful to create this inventory of documents and focus areas as a template, to provide the project team with a list of documents that are being requested and reviewed, and have them prepare the list as part of the planning process.

3.4 Plan for logistics

Lastly, once the assessment plan is developed and the inventories of documents and interviews are created, the assessment logistics need to be finalized and planned for. There are many logistics to prepare, and these activities may seem somewhat administrative in nature, but proper logistics can be the difference between a smooth assessment and a rough one. For example, not having meeting rooms for interviews, or not having access to project documents on a locked site, can slow down the assessment process. Below are some logistics to consider and prepare for when planning the project assessment.

- **Project assessment**
  - ○ Have a central repository for assessment files where the review team can access documents in an organized structure.
  - ○ Create a contact list for assessment team members with key contact information, such as email and phone numbers.
  - ○ Consider having security on particular assessment files, if appropriate. For example, password protect key documents which may contain financial information or candid interview feedback.
  - ○ Access and IDs for assessment team members if not part of the corporation where the project is being assessed.
  - ○ Schedule a kickoff meeting with project team members to review the objectives, approach and plan.
- **Project documents**
  - ○ Determine the approach for storing and retrieving project documents which could include a separate repository.
  - ○ Obtain access to file shares for team members, as some sites may require users to be set up to view documents.
  - ○ Understand email protocols, as some corporations have limits on the size of attachments which can be sent, or security around specific information contained within emails or documents.

- **Team member interviews**
  - o Determine the location to conduct team member interviews which could include meeting at the project location site, a conference room at the corporation, or a separate location away from the corporation.
  - o Schedule meeting rooms if conducting team member interviews at the location of the project.
  - o Confirm access to the building for the interviews, or that someone will meet you to let you in.
  - o Ensure that meeting invitations get sent so people being interviewed know the time and location.
  - o Have dial-in numbers for conference calls and include them in meeting invitations for team member interviews.

Once the plans have been developed, including planning for interviewing team members, reviewing documents and logistics, the assessment can begin. Before the collection of information can be started, several initial activities are important to ensure a smooth start to the assessment. First, is that a message should come out from a senior executive announcing the assessment, along with the intent, timing and activities. This will provide the assessment team with the right level of support as they start reaching out to team members for information. Secondly, an initial kickoff meeting should be conducted with key team members to walk through the details of the assessment and set expectations for timing, who will be interviewed, what documents will be reviewed, and the key milestones for the assessment, including the timing of the final report.

CHAPTER 4: COLLECT INFORMATION

Once the plans are developed and the assessment is under way, pertinent project information can be collected. This is a very important step because the key to a successful assessment is collecting the right project information which will reveal the trends, themes and gaps. Information can be gathered from both interviews and documents, and so the approach for collecting it may be iterative, as documents can identify more interview questions and interviews may yield more documents to look at.

The following sections in this chapter are dedicated to each of the different project management functions to be assessed. There are five subsections for each of the functions which will be used to describe the function, and provide some suggestions for areas to focus on, and items for consideration.

1. *Description and value* – a description of the function, along with the value of that function to project delivery.
2. *Key roles and focus areas* – identifies the key roles associated to each function, as well as relevant questions to ask during the interviews.
3. *Key documents and focus areas* – identifies the key project documents to look for and gather, and suggested focus areas for each.
4. *Considerations* – some insights and relevant points to consider when collecting information for each function.
5. *Case study* – a real world case study highlighting a project assessment that focused on the function, along

with findings and lessons learned.

4.1 Project structure and governance

4.1.1 Description and value

The first area to focus on during the project assessment should be on the structure and governance which is the foundation for how a project is set up, organized and run. Understanding the structure will also provide the context for the assessment team as to how the project is organized, and who the key team members and stakeholders are. A logical and clear project structure results in clarity of accountabilities, transparency of work across the project and programs, and a higher probability of success.

Structure is even more important with programs because they tend to be comprised of multiple projects, and require roles and management that span across those projects. Most programs are set up as a matrix of key roles and functions. *Figure 4.1* demonstrates a classic program matrix by showing the projects as vertical functions and the domains as horizontal functions, with the team members at the intersections. Notice how each role is accountable for the delivery of the project that they are on (vertical), as well as to ensure consistency and that they work across projects (horizontal). Most programs also have a dedicated program management office, or PMO, which manages the operations of the program, such as financials, resources, vendor contracts and communications.

Program Office	Project 1		Project 2	
Business Lead	Business Analyst	Business Analyst	Business Analyst	Business Analyst
	Business Rules	Business Workflow	Business Rules	Business Workflow
Technical Lead	Technical Architect	Platform Architect	Technical Architect	Platform Architect
	Developer	Developer	Developer	Developer
Testing Lead	Test Planning	Test Planning	Test Planning	Test Planning
	Test Execution	Test Execution	Test Execution	Test Execution

Figure 4.1: Program matrix

Beyond the structure of the IT roles within the project, it is also important to have alignment between the business and IT role. The Institute for Internal Auditors defines business alignment well (IIA, 2009); "...vision and objectives of both the business and IT are understood, are in harmony with each other, and that the project is in line with the strategy of the organization." So, the project assessment should look to understand if there is business and IT alignment and clarity of the roles and responsibilities between the different organizations.

The structure defines how a project is organized but governance defines how the project is managed. Project governance includes everything from executive sponsorship to steering committee meetings, phase gates and document sign offs. Governance should be clear and well defined so the team understands how the work is managed, and when to engage corporation and project leadership.

4.1.2 Key roles and focus areas

Since structure and governance span across the project, there are several different roles which should be considered for interview.

- Project manager
  - Discuss how the project is structured and governed, including the key project roles and interface points.
  - Discuss alignment of business and IT roles and responsibilities, and any concerns or gaps.
  - Discuss how the business case, objectives and goals are being communicated and managed within the project.
  - Discuss how well the project is following the documented approach within the charter, business case and project management approach.
- IT lead
  - Discuss how the project is structured and governed.
  - Discuss alignment of business and IT roles and responsibilities, and any concerns or gaps.
- Business lead
  - Discuss how the project is structured and governed.
  - Discuss alignment of business and IT roles and responsibilities, and any concerns or gaps.
- Team members
  - Get their perspectives on how well the project is organized, structured and governed.

- o Get their perspectives on the clarity of the roles and responsibilities within the project structure.
- o Get their perspectives on the clarity of business case, objectives, and priorities and alignment to their work.

4.1.3 Key documents and focus areas

There are several project documents which should identify the business case, project structure and project governance. These should be reviewed to gain insight into the approach for the structure and governance approach for the project.

- Business case
  - o Confirm that this includes the business problem, priorities, and objectives for the project.
  - o Should identify who the customers of the project results are.
  - o Should include the expected quantified and non-quantified business benefits from the realization of the project goals.
  - o Should be approved and signed off by key project stakeholders and leaders.
- Project charter
  - o Confirm that the charter includes the objectives, benefits, high level milestones, priorities, and team structure, with the key roles.
  - o Should include the structure and responsibilities between the business and IT teams.
  - o Should be approved and signed off, and used to communicate the project to new team members or other interested stakeholders.

- Project management approach
  - ○ Confirm that the project management approach is documented and includes the key functions to managing a project (project management methodology, issue management, risk management, communications approach and other operational items).
  - ○ Should identify the approach for governing the project, including steering committee meetings, phase reviews/gates, reviews and sign offs, and senior management engagement.
  - ○ Should be communicated to the team so that expectations are clear as to how the project will be managed.

4.1.4 Considerations

There are several factors to be aware of when reviewing the project structure and governance; all of which are very important in how the team is organized and aligned around the business case and charter of the project.

Alignment around objectives

It is essential to have clarity of business problems, objectives and priorities, and ensure that the project team is aware of them. The team needs to be aligned to these, so that they understand the context and priority of their work. It also helps them to feel a sense of purpose for their work, aligned to larger corporation objectives. It is not enough to have these buried in a document somewhere; they need to be well communicated and in many places to "ground" team members with their purpose and value.

Alignment of deliverables

It is important to then align the deliverables to the project objectives, as well as consider the benefits and customers of the project. This sets the context for the deliverable and keeps the perspective for how the deliverable should be used. It also grounds all of the project deliverables to the same objectives. For example, if the objectives are to deliver a capability by a specific date, then these milestones should be identified in major project documents, and be tracked towards in team meetings.

Business and IT alignment

Most technology projects have business components as well as technology components. There can often be confusion around accountabilities between business roles and IT roles, so this is an important area to look into during the assessment. For example, some projects have both business and IT project managers so, in this case, the division of responsibilities should be documented and well understood.

Right amount of attention

How a project is governed has a significant impact on the outcomes of that project and therefore proper focus should be given to this area during the project assessment. If key stakeholders are not engaged sufficiently, or sign offs of key documents are not performed, there could be challenges later to the project in the form of rework, additional cost, missed or misunderstood business requirements, or even failing to meet the project objectives.

Clarity of structure

Projects that are not structured well have problems with role clarity, accountability and morale, and inevitably will struggle to meet commitments. These impacts are magnified on larger projects and programs, so it is important to ensure that the structure is set up properly and that the team is clear on it, and is operating within that model.

4.1.5 Case study

A program made of a collection of loosely managed projects with not much cross-project structure

While working as an internal consultant for a Fortune 100 corporation, I was asked by the chief technology officer (who I was working for at the time) to review a $16 million program that he was the IT lead for. The program had been running for several months but did not seem to be making enough progress or have transparency of the risks. He was getting a status report every week which showed a green status but he was sensing that this was not an accurate reflection of the program, and he asked me to perform an assessment. I pulled together the approach and plan for a four week program assessment which included interviewing several key program team members and stakeholders, as well as reviewing all of the program documents in the central repository.

Before interviewing anyone from the program team, I gathered and reviewed many key documents and found several consistent themes emerging which indicated not having a well-defined or organized program structure. This theme was then validated as I spoke to several program team members comprised of the leads, project managers, business analysts and technical team resources.

After the collection of information, I had documented several pervasive themes. The overarching theme was that the program was really organized as a set of discretely managed projects which were grouped loosely under the name of a program but were certainly not managed as one. Some examples are listed below:

- Not many program level deliverables including plans, organization charts, resource rosters, risk logs or financial reports. When packaging the assessment report I used a "heat map" to document all key project management deliverables and then demonstrate which project-level deliverables existed (green colored) and where the program level deliverables were either incomplete (yellow) or did not exist at all (red). This was an effective visual to highlight the discrepancy with the documents and demonstrate the point that there were not many program deliverables.

- Minimal clarity of program roles. The teams were working almost as independent projects and so there was no clear understanding of roles at the program level, nor were there many people working across projects. There was also no clear program escalation point, which came across consistently in several interviews, as team members did not know who to raise issues to, who to escalate to when further action was needed, or who to work with to push for decisions to be made.

- The program was referred to by different names. In program documentation, the program was referred to as three different names. No wonder the program team members and stakeholders were confused.

- Scope was not captured in one place. Since the projects were acting independently, even the aggregate scope was hard to find in one place, and was stored in several disparate documents and shared project folders. This also perpetuated the perception of not being one program and the confusion of the work to be done.

- Status was reported out at the individual project level and not at the program level, so there was not one package of information for stakeholders to get an overall sense of the program health.

Based on these findings regarding the program structure, I suggested a set of recommendations to restructure the work to be managed as one program, with one name, and to develop clarity of roles and scope. The following recommendations were proposed as part of the program assessment final report:

- Restructure the work as specific projects under one program, and define roles that span across the projects. This proposed program structure looked very similar to the one documented in *Figure 4.1*. The action was to define and document this structure, as well as the roles and responsibilities.

- Have the team revalidate the plans across the projects, focused on identifying dependencies between them. This would identify any deliverables, or milestones, which were to be tracked at the program level.

- Create program level deliverables, such as the program management approach, including specifics for how the program will be managed, a centralized scope repository, and the integrated program plan.

After seeing the assessment results and recommendations which validated their perceptions, the CTO and business sponsor decided to have me take over as the program manager and perform the restructuring, as well as deliver on the program commitments. Note that I am not sure that I wanted to be "rewarded" from having a solid assessment by being given the program to manage. It did take several months but we reorganized the team, renamed the program, developed program and project plans, and rallied the team around the program goals. As a result, the program managed to complete its work and added the expected value to the corporation. It even won an industry award for technology innovation which was a satisfying recognition of the program turnaround.

4.2 Scope and change management

4.2.1 Description and value

The starting point for every project is with the identification of the work to be completed (i.e. the scope). This includes capturing all capabilities and business requirements that are necessary to complete the project and meet its objectives. Scope can be managed at different levels of detail, from high level scope statements down to detailed specifications, capabilities and requirements. Each scope element should be aligned to a specific project and have resources, cost and schedule milestones associated to it. Then, once scope is defined, a change management process needs to be established, and followed, to ensure that changes to scope get assessed, tracked and managed diligently.

Figure 4.2 demonstrates the high level process for scope and change management, starting with the documentation of project scope (Step 1) and then the collection of detailed requirements (Step 2).

```
┌────────────────┐   ┌────────────────┐   ┌──────────────────┐
│  1. Document   │   │  2. Develop    │   │ 3. Review, Approve│
│     Scope      │──▶│   Detailed     │──▶│      and         │──┐
│                │   │  Requirements  │   │  Baseline Scope   │  │
└────────────────┘   └────────────────┘   └──────────────────┘  │
         ┌───────────────────────────────────────────────────────┘
         ▼
┌────────────────┐   ┌────────────────┐   ┌──────────────────┐
│  4. Identify   │   │ 5. Assess Impact│   │  6. Decide on    │
│    Change      │──▶│   of Change    │──▶│   Disposition    │──┐
│                │   │                │   │                  │  │
└────────────────┘   └────────────────┘   └──────────────────┘  │
         ┌───────────────────────────────────────────────────────┘
         ▼
┌────────────────┐
│  7. Update     │
│  Documents     │
│                │
└────────────────┘
```

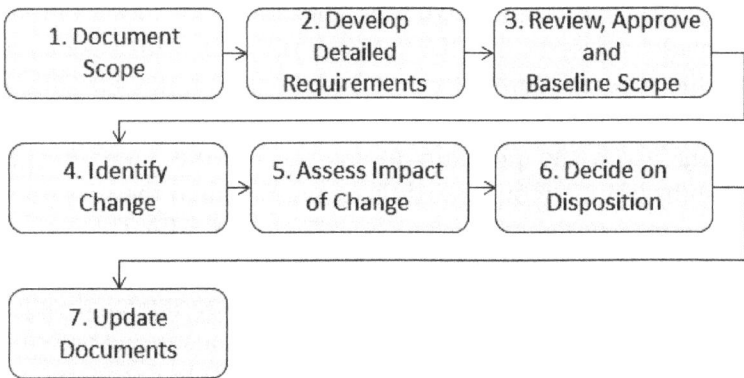

Figure 4.2: Scope and change management process

After the project scope is identified and documented it should be reviewed, and approved, by business experts and leadership (Step 3). This is a critical step, as there is a cascading impact of changes to scope as the project progresses along the delivery timeline, so the scope should be reviewed carefully early on. Changes become much more impactful to cost and schedule the later they are found because of the rework associated with those changes. Once scope is approved and baselined, a change management process can be used to control changes to the scope, and the implications of those changes as they get identified (Steps 4-6). The last step is ensuring that any project documents get updated as a result of the change control, to ensure that project documents stay current (Step 7).

The term "change management" can have several meanings with relation to projects. For the purposes of this chapter, the term will refer to managing the changes in project scope, and not preparing an organization for changes that the project will introduce. Change management is an important function to running a project because it puts controls around the scope, schedule and cost of a program.

Assumptions will change as the project progresses but it is critical to assess the impacts of those changes and then make informed decisions on how to proceed. This process helps to manage expectations of stakeholders, instead of seeing what appear to be random fluctuations in project schedule or cost.

Scope and change management become more significant for programs than for projects because of the complexity and size associated with programs. Programs may have many scope elements which span across projects and need to be carefully managed and tracked. Also, because programs are larger than projects, change management is needed because of the large number of moving parts which need to be managed and controlled, as well as assessed for impact from the changes.

4.2.2 Key roles and focus areas

The interviews for the assessment should focus on the approach to capture, document, review, approve and baseline the scope for the project, as well as how changes to that scope get assessed and managed.

- Business lead
  - o Confirm that there is clarity of project scope for the project and no open clarifications are required.
  - o Discuss their view of the scope management and change management processes on the project.
- Project manager and PMO
  - o Discuss how scope is managed and documented on the project.
  - o Discuss the approach for reviews and sign offs of requirements and other scope documents.

- o Discuss if the change control approach is documented and understood including impact assessments, tracking changes and updating project documents.
- Business analyst
  - o Discuss how scope is documented and managed including templates, tools used and reporting.
  - o Confirm that the right business experts are aligned to the project and available when needed.
  - o Confirm that the review and approval process is adequate including the identification of key business resources to perform these.
- Subject matter expert
  - o Confirm how the subject matter experts are leveraged to facilitate requirements and get their perspectives on how well this is managed.
  - o Get perspectives on scope reviews and sign offs.

4.2.3 Key documents and focus areas

The project documents should provide clarity around the scope management and change management approaches, as well as include centralized locations for project scope, requirements and changes.

- Scope management approach
  - o Documented approach for managing, tracking and signing off on scope and requirements.
  - o Clear identification of who is reviewing and signing off on scope and business requirements.
  - o Aligns with corporation standard framework and processes for managing scope and requirements.

- Centralized scope repository
  - o Project scope documented in one location and maintained in a repository.
  - o Reviews and approval of scope documented.
  - o It may be helpful to look for some examples of completed scope documents with reviews and approvals, to understand the level of rigor used to manage scope documents.
- Change management approach
  - o Document approach for identifying, assessing, estimating and deciding on changes, including the approval process.
  - o Approach for updating documents once change is approved, to ensure that they stay current.
- Change log
  - o Confirm that all proposed and approved changes are managed and tracked in a central location.
  - o The change log should include key information, such as a description of the change, person or team proposing it, impact of the change if implemented (e.g. costs, benefits, resources, schedule, etc.), and the disposition (e.g. approved, rejected, deferred).

4.2.4 Considerations

Correctly managing scope on a project is at the core of controlling the project variables, such as schedule and cost. This is because scope drives the work, duration of the activities, complexity of the technology solution, resources required and the cost of the project. Also, changes can arise at any time and add cost and scope to the project which also will have implications on the project. The assessment should take this into account and look into how scope and changes are managed and controlled. Some considerations for assessing the management of scope are documented below.

Single source of truth

Project scope should be documented and stored in one central location so it can be easily referenced by team members and there is no confusion as to what is in or out of scope. The project team should have a central tool, or repository, to store scope elements; which can also be useful for tracing those scope items to other deliverables in later phases of the delivery lifecycle (such as testing). Each of these scope elements should also be tied back to specific project objectives or goals. This single source of truth should also be viewed as "living" and therefore be updated as changes in scope are identified, so that it always has a current view of project requirements.

Requires diligence to maintain

Because everything on the project ties back to the scope, it is important to keep the scope documents maintained. This means ensuring that scope statements are well documented and stay current as changes are introduced. A good way to do this is to have a checklist of key project documents that must be updated after a change is approved. For example, a change in project scope could result in updates to master scope documents, the project charter, requirements documents, the project schedule and milestones, project cost documents and testing documents. Each of these needs to be maintained as scope evolves, or they can become outdated and incorrect which could lead to problems with project delivery, quality or customer satisfaction.

Consider level of detail

Scope can be documented at varying degrees of granularity from high level scope statements (e.g. I want a computer) to very low levels of details (e.g. the computer should be blue with 2GB of memory and 20GB of storage). Some projects and corporation frameworks define, and use, a taxonomy which defines the structure from high level to low level scope. Note that the more detailed that the scope is, the less room there is for interpretation mistakes. The assessment should be aware of the level of detail in the scope, and look to see if that is adequate for the project.

Static requirements vs scenarios

Scope can be organized in many different ways, from listing of specific capabilities to scenarios (also known as use cases). Scenarios tend to be a better way to organize scope because they document specific flows, show alternative paths and identify key linkage points. Documenting a list of requirements may lose some of this context and even miss important elements. The assessment should pay attention to how the scope is documented and see if scenarios are appropriate for the project being reviewed.

Ensure reviews and sign offs

It is very important to ensure that project scope documents get reviewed and signed off by empowered business experts and leads. Inevitably on every project there will be disputes on what is actually in scope, and the team will get into the "what I meant" vs "what was documented" debate. There are also significant implications to changes late in projects, in the form of missed milestones, added cost and rework.

Having reviews and sign offs should allow for detailed discussions early on, and a documented audit trail of what was actually approved. This could also reduce the risk of rework and late surprises. The assessment should look closely at the review and approval process for scope, as well as get some examples of these documents.

Consider downstream linkages

Although scope is defined early in the project, it sets the foundation for the entirety of the project. Well managed projects trace scope from requirements through to design specifications, coding documents and testing conditions. This allows projects to validate that the original defined scope was delivered through to completion. This is also important during the testing phases, to ensure that each scenario was tested which results in higher quality outcomes. This traceability may be something to look at during the project assessment.

Changes have implications

Projects spend a lot of time on planning for the work including documenting the scope, estimating the work, and developing the associated schedules and budgets. As assumptions or scope elements change on the project, it is important to assess the implications of these changes on those primary project documents, and then update them accordingly when changes get approved. This could include additional cost, the need for more resources and schedule changes based on dependencies to changing milestones. The assessment should look for this level of impact analysis and process to keep documents updated as part of the change management process.

4.2.5 Case study

Lack of rigor around documenting, tracing and changing scope

At one time in my career, I was managing the Capability Maturity Model Integration (CMMI) organization for a Fortune 100 corporation. This is an industry standard approach for managing the delivery of IT projects and application development. We had established the IT delivery framework which included a series of project quality reviews, to ensure quality of delivery and compliance to corporation standards. Our team was asked to assess a large program in one of the business segments, focused specifically on reviewing three areas; scope management, project management and architecture.

We interviewed several of the program team members, spanning many roles within business and technology, and also reviewed the key program documentation. After the initial analysis was completed, there were 22 risk areas related to the management of scope which were identified and documented. Some of the more significant findings included the following examples:

- Scope was not finalized or baselined so it was not clear what the full set of requirements were for the program. This was demonstrated in comments from the team and the documentation not being comprehensive.

- The team was using the standard tools and processes for documentation of project requirements.

- Scope was documented in several different locations and there was no centrally stored repository. This led to confusion from the team members as to the official list of what was in scope.

- Requirements traceability did not exist within the program delivery (e.g. to design documents and test cases). Therefore, it was hard to tell if the requirements were being delivered through the stages of the project lifecycle.

- The change management process was lightly documented but not formally structured, or being used consistently. This resulted in a lack of understanding of the history of changes and financial variances which could not be easily explained.

As a result of these findings, the assessment team documented several recommendations including the development of a plan to complete scope and requirement documentation. There were also recommendations around centrally managing scope within the corporation standard tool, for requirements which could also be used to trace scope throughout the program delivery lifecycle. Lastly, the assessment suggested establishing a more rigorous and defined change management process, to control the volatility of scope.

This assessment was conducted during the early stages of the program which allowed the program team to implement these recommendations before the impact of those findings became more significant. Additional follow up reviews were conducted which validated that these actions were performed.

4.3 Schedule management

4.3.1 Description and value

The project schedule is probably the most critical tool that a project manager has to use because it identifies the full body of work required to complete the project, it highlights the key dependencies within that work and the delivery milestones, it aligns the activities to the resources that are performing the work, and is also used to manage and track progress against deliverables and milestones. While there are definitional differences between a project schedule and a project plan, for the purposes of this section they will be used interchangeably to reference the detailed list of all project milestones, phases, activities and tasks.

There are many benefits for a project by having a well organized and maintained project schedule.

- The project work is documented in one place. This allows the project manager to manage the many moving parts of the project, or program, including dependencies between projects and external to the project.

- The team can model out the duration of the project based on activities, activity duration and dependencies between activities.

- Keeping the schedule updated provides transparency into expectations and gives project team members something to work towards. Without dates and expectation setting, the natural tendency of people is to not feel a sense of urgency, and therefore, milestones will be missed.

- The project manager can track how they are progressing against project milestones and goals. This allows for corrective action to be taken, based on early indications of progress or trends.

- Team members can look at the plan to understand what activities they are assigned to, and the expectations for when to complete them.

- Impacts of changes, or issues, can be understood based on dependencies and durations of activities.

Schedule management is even more important for programs because of the interdependencies between projects within a program. As *Figure 4.3* shows, a project schedule could be organized by the project phases, deliverables, milestones and activities. A program schedule is a rollup of the projects with their phases, key deliverables and dependencies. The program may also document the interproject dependencies, such as the line shown on the bottom of the diagram depicting a dependency between activities.

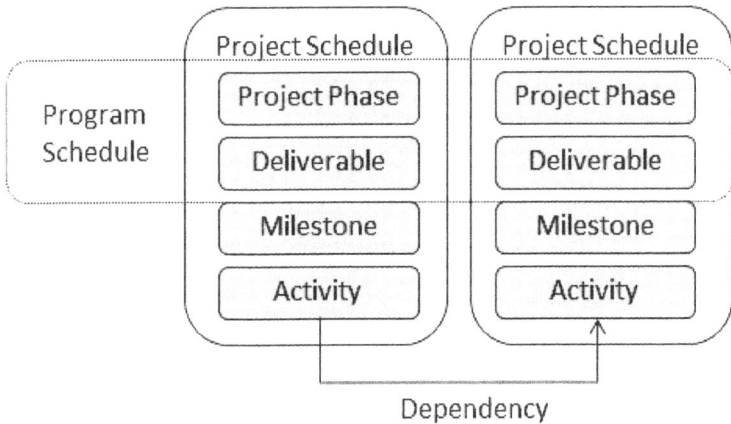

Figure 4.3: Program and project schedules

Because of the importance of the schedule, the project assessment should not just look to see if a plan exists, but should look at how the plan is being managed and how work is being tracked, and reported, against commitments. The schedule should be viewed as a "living" document which gets updated and maintained regularly, so that it always has a current view of the project status against commitments.

4.3.2 Key roles and focus areas

The interviews should focus on the project team members who are managing the plans (project managers), team members who contribute to the plan, as well as team members who are "customers" of the plan information, such as business customers, dependent projects or project sponsors.

- IT lead and sponsor
  - Confirm proper communication of milestones, critical path and progress against schedule commitments.
- Project manager
  - Discuss how the project schedule was created with activities, durations and milestones.
  - Confirm that there is a formal project plan with activities, dates, names and durations.
  - Discuss how the project plan information is tracked and updated on a regular basis.
  - Discuss what techniques are used to monitor and report on plan progress (e.g. earned value, percentage complete, etc.).
  - Discuss how the project is tracking to its schedule commitments.
  - Discuss how changes and issues get modelled to understand impacts on milestones.
- PMO
  - Discuss the approach for schedule creation, management, tracking and reporting.
  - Discuss alignment of change management and schedule management.
- Team members
  - Discuss how they contributed to the creation of the plan and activities, as well as the updating of activity progress.

o Ask if they are aware of the key activities, milestone dates and progress of the plan.

4.3.3 Key documents and focus areas

The documents reviewed for schedule management should include the approach, as well as a thorough assessment of the project plans.

- Schedule management approach
  - o Document approach for developing the schedule and activities based on estimates and planning.
  - o Document approach for how to manage schedules, activities, dependencies, tracking progress and reporting on activity progress.
  - o Document how to assess schedule impacts of risks, issues and changes.
  - o For programs, document approach for how to manage the schedule across projects, manage dependencies, and rollup progress from project plans into a program plan.
- Project plan
  - o Plan should be developed and maintained in corporation standard tools, where they are identified.
  - o Plan should include the deliverables and milestones from the corporation standard SDLC framework, where it exists.
  - o Plan should be organized and well structured into logical groupings of work, with their associated activities and tasks.
  - o Plan should contain milestones, phases, activities, dates, names and task durations.
  - o Dependencies are identified, and included, in the plan (internal and external to the project).

○ Contains the critical path for the project.
○ Plans are maintained (e.g. milestones past due are either marked as complete, or reforecast to new dates).
○ Review the plans to understand what the progress is against schedule commitments.
• Dependency matrix
○ Dependencies are identified and tracked (within the project, across projects within a program and external to the project or program).
○ The type of activity dependencies are identified, such as start-finish where activity two starts after activity one finishes, or start-start where both activities start at the same time.

4.3.4 Considerations

The assessment should plan to spend a good amount of time on the management of the project schedule, since this is a key indicator of project progress and clarity of work, and represents diligence in project management.

Look for a structured breakdown

A project schedule should be based on a defined structure of work which breaks down into logical components. Most industry materials on schedules refer to this as a "work breakdown structure." This structure can be based on the logical SDLC phases, such as phases and deliverables within those phases, or the sequential set of activities required to complete a deliverable. Because plans can span thousands of line items, it is important to ensure that the activities are well organized and easy to find and manage.

Understand tracking techniques

Having a project plan is only valuable if it gets maintained and tracked. The assessment should look at how the plan is being managed and updated. For example, look to see how progress is being measured, such as percent complete, or "earning" completion, as a particular task is finished. More complex schedule management techniques can include earned value management (EVM) which is a sophisticated method of tracking expected completion of activities compared to planned progress.

Maintenance of plans

A key indicator of how well a project is being managed is in how well the project plan is maintained. For example, project activities that are past their completion date should be either marked as 100% complete, or updated with a new target completion date. Other examples include keeping the activities and dates updated as plan changes get identified, or as dependencies get updated.

Plans that are not well maintained can be indicative of not having strong project management discipline which may also be a theme in other facets of the project. Plans should be the anchor for the entire team to understand the work, and the progress against that, so ample time should be spent in keeping them maintained.

Dependencies are understood

As projects become more complex and increase in size, dependency management is becoming a very useful practice. Projects should identify dependencies within their plans and with other projects (which may be within a program or external). Dependencies become important as schedules change, or as risks and issues get identified, so that an impact assessment can be made to understand the implications of those possible changes.

Baseline the plan

It is good practice to baseline a project plan early in the project. This is when a project completes the plan and then "locks" in the milestones and dates as the official commitments of the projects. Then, as any changes get identified, they can be tracked and updated (but the baseline does not change). This also allows the project to have an audit history of original dates, and updated dates, based on approved changes.

Teams should be involved

The plan should be developed based on input from the team members, since they are most likely the ones performing the activities, and would be best qualified to provide realistic timelines and steps needed to complete the work. Having them involved in the creation of the plan also helps them to buy into the milestones and dates, as opposed to feeling like they are being given the dates from management.

The project team should always be aware of the milestone activities and dates that they are working toward, and therefore the plan should be communicated and shared on a frequent basis. This could mean including key milestones in a weekly status report, or using the plan as an agenda item in team meetings.

Manage the schedule "left to right"

In many projects, the timelines are set before the team starts detailed planning, meaning that they have to create the schedule by working backwards from the committed to end date (from "right to left" on the schedule). This could include compliance projects which have a fixed completion date, or a business commitment to a customer, or the marketplace, which has already been communicated.

Ideally, schedules should be created from "left to right" based on the activities, duration of those activities, and dependencies which would identify what the end date really should be. When there are fixed timelines, the assessment team should look at the feasibility of making those timelines, and determine if any action is needed to increase the probability of meeting those milestones (e.g. removing scope).

Manageable work units

In order to track progress properly, it is important to have small units of work, with short durations, on the project plan. Some industry best practices believe that there should not be any activities on a plan with durations greater than two to four weeks. Anything larger than this would be too difficult to gage progress on, and should be broken down into smaller components for better tracking purposes.

Consider schedule contingency

Since every project has unexpected events and assumptions change, a project manager may want to consider adding some contingency to their schedule. This means adding in a week, or two, at specific points in the schedule between milestones, to allow for the absorption of schedule slippage. This approach is an effective way of providing some schedule "buffer" should problems arise (which often occurs). Many times this is not possible given tight schedules, but this is a good technique for projects that have risk, or many unknowns, to allow some time for unplanned activities.

Utilize a standard tool

There are many project planning tools in the marketplace which facilitate activity planning, resource alignment and dependency management. Utilizing a tool can be beneficial, especially for larger and more complex projects which have many activities, milestones and interdependencies. Some corporations may have standard tools, or templates, and this may also be up to the discretion of the project manager.

4.3.5 Case study

Just having a program plan is not sufficient

I was asked to conduct an assessment for a program at a Property & Casualty corporation which cost tens of millions of US dollars of investment money. While many areas of the program were reviewed, it was the schedule management function where the most significant findings and recommendations were documented. This program had created a program plan but it had many deficiencies in it. Some examples are below:

- The team did not contribute to coming up with the activities, durations, or dates, so there was not much credibility and buy in with the plan or the milestones.

- The team was not aware of what the schedule was and therefore the milestones that they were working towards, so there was not a sense of urgency to complete work, since there were no clear expectations of timing.

- Some milestones were documented at the program level but they were not assigned to owners, and were not being tracked.

- The dates in the plan did not match the standard technology release milestones that the corporation maintained.

- Some dependencies between deliverables were identified but they were tracked in a separate document and not in the program plan.

- There were 63 activities on the plan which had dates which were past date and not marked as complete, or with updated dates. It was hard to tell if these activities were actually completed and the plan was not updated, or if these had moved past their dates, in which case an assessment of impact would be needed.

- Some activities on the plan had very long durations including one task which was 140 days in duration. This made it very hard to track and report progress against the commitment dates.

Given the identified challenges, it was no surprise that this program was struggling to meet its commitments. There were many risks, project sponsors could not easily interpret the progress, and team morale was low. Several recommendations were identified to restructure the plan and then manage it better going forward. The first recommendation was to reforecast the plan based on realistic timelines which required involving the team's input on activities, durations and dependencies.

The next recommendation was to baseline the schedule and then communicate it to the team. In fact, once the plan was completed, it was published on large printer paper and then pasted on the walls of the team work area. Now no one on the team could say that they did not know the milestones or important dates, since they could see them from their workstation.

Lastly, a tracking and reporting approach was created to ensure that the plan was maintained, and progress was communicated to stakeholders. This included updating the status report with milestone information including dates, percent complete, and health of that milestone, with associated risks and issues.

These recommendations were implemented over a period of weeks and months, and with this renewed structure and focus on the schedule, the team was able to deliver on the revised plan. The team morale also picked up because the team felt involved in the planning, and had clarity of expectations and goals for the program. Lastly, the sponsors were happy because there was better transparency into the progress and risks of the program, and they could see where decisions or actions could be taken.

In this example, the program manager had developed a plan but it was not sufficient for the assessment to just "check the box" that the plan existed but rather get into the details of how it was created, how it is used, and how it is tracked. Focusing on the structure of the plan and how it was being managed, allowed for the assessment to yield significantly improved results on the program and for the corporation.

4.4 Cost management

4.4.1 Description and value

The prior sections of this chapter focused on the management of the scope of the project and the schedule for delivery. The next logical progression to look at is the management of cost which is essentially comprised of the resources and materials required to meet the scope and schedule for the projects. On projects, there are typically four different types of costs which are highlighted in *Table 4.1* with examples.

Table 4.1: Types of technology project costs

Type of Cost	Description	Examples
Internal Resources	Resources working on the project who are from within the organization that is sponsoring the project	• Employees, such as project managers, business analysts or developers
External Resources	Resources working on the project who are from outside the organization that is sponsoring the program, including specialized contractors	• Contracted resources (either fixed bid or variable cost) • Consulting corporations • Software consultants or integrators
Material Costs	Acquisition of materials required to meet project objectives	• Hardware costs • Software licenses
Operating Costs	Additional expenses incurred to run the project	• Travel expenses • Office supplies • Training fees

Each of the project cost types listed above need to be estimated, managed, tracked and reported at a detailed level over the duration of the project. Each of these dimensions of cost management should be reviewed during the assessment. Because corporations are making significant dollar investments into projects, the management of the financials is an important aspect to the project and the corporation.

Estimation

The assessment should look into how project estimates are created, as these are the starting point for cost management, and set the expectations for how much the project will cost to deliver. Estimates are also used to make business decisions around priorities within the portfolio and what to fund. The Project Management Institute identifies the importance of estimating (PMI 2010); "Project estimating activities are a relatively small part of the overall project plan …However, effective project estimating is a key contributor to the successful planning and delivery of project objectives."

There are a few common approaches for developing project cost forecasts. Three of them are documented below:

- *Bottom up* – this approach is based on building the estimate from the "bottom up", based on activities, resources and the duration of work. In this case, the cost can be assigned to resources based on their labor cost, multiplied by their assigned allocation and duration on the project.

- *Parametric models* – this approach is where estimates are generated based on specific units of work that are given a complexity score and estimate based on that score. Examples include Function Point analysis or Use Case Complexity scoring.

- *Analogous estimates* – this approach compares the project to other projects with similar scope, duration, technology solution, or complexity, to determine the estimate.

It is considered a best practice to use multiple estimation models, and then compare the results to calibrate the estimates. Team involvement is also a consideration for estimates, since involving team members in the process can yield more accurate estimates and better buy-in for the results and plan. Lastly, programs that have multiple projects, and span multiple years, should consider a process to maintain estimation models and calibrate them based on actual results from historical projects.

Tracking and managing

After reviewing how estimates are developed, the assessment should then look into how project costs are forecasted, managed and tracked. This can include the processes, tools and documents used by the project manager and project management office. Most corporations have existing standards and tools for how to manage project costs, capture actual incurred costs, and report on results and variances to budgets. The following are examples of activities involved in tracking and managing project costs:

- The budget for the project grouped by cost type (labor, consultants, contracts, infrastructure and operating expenses) and allocated to the months of the program. This is usually locked down and does not change.
- Updated forecasts based on changes in assumptions, approved change controls and actual costs to date.
- Tracking the inventory of approved change controls and their associated impact of financial forecasts.

- Tracking of actual incurred costs by cost type and month.

- Tracking of variances between the budget and actual costs, organized by cost type and month.

- Tracking of budget, forecast and actuals by organization. Many projects include resources from different organizations, and organizations account for resources by expense center, so it may be important to align project costs to expense centers.

- Tracking of contract information for vendors including cost expected payments and invoices.

- A calendar of the financial management process used by the project including when forecasts get locked in, when actual costs get reported, and when financial variance reports are due.

- Tracking of depreciation and capitalization. Most corporations have financial organizations to manage this separately from project cost management but, at the very least, the project needs to work with this organization to identify which assets can be capitalized or depreciated.

This list demonstrates that there are many different activities required in the management and tracking of financial information. The project should have a clearly documented approach for financial management, and then follow that to ensure that project finances are being managed properly.

Reporting

Lastly, project managers should have a set of reports which are used to communicate the financial health of the project.

These reports should come out on a regular cadence and include transparency of key financial information for the stakeholders of the project. Projects should document the approach and calendar of reporting, with planned frequencies and formats. Some examples of these reports are listed below.

- Budget and forecast by cost type and month.
- Actual cost compared to budget and forecast by cost type and month. This is usually a monthly report when actual costs get reported.
- Cost reporting for resources by expense center or organization.
- Variance identification and explanation.
- Approved change controls with impact to forecast and actual costs.
- On programs, detailed cost information by project and in aggregate.

For programs, cost management should be considered an aggregation of project cost management. In this case, costs need to be understood, and managed, at the project level but then also rolled up at the program level. Programs also tend to have specific program level costs for those resources and expenditures which span across projects, such as a program management office (PMO) or an overall testing lead. Tracking and reporting should be conducted at the project and program levels.

4.4.2 Key roles and focus areas

The interviews for cost management should focus on the approach for managing costs and how that aligns with corporation standards, as well as looking at how costs are being managed on the project.

- PMO
  - o Discuss the approach for developing project estimates including the involvement of the team.
  - o Discuss the approach for managing financials including forecasting for all of the cost types, capturing and tracking actual costs, conducting variance analysis and reporting.
  - o Discuss the approach for management reporting including variance explanations and approvals for cost overruns.
  - o Discuss the approach for cost management in the change control process including updating financial documents.
- Project manager
  - o Discuss how the project estimates were developed.
  - o Discuss how project financials are managed including forecasting for all of the cost types, capturing and tracking actual costs, conducting variance analysis and reporting.
  - o Discuss how cost is managed in the change control process.
  - o Review how the project is tracking against the budget and any current financial reporting.
- IT lead and business lead
  - o Get their perspectives on how well the project financials and estimates are managed.
  - o Confirm that they are getting the right level of transparency into project financials and financial health.

- Team members
  - Discuss the involvement of the team in the creation of estimates and management of financials.

4.4.3 Key documents and focus areas

The documents reviewed should outline the approach for managing costs on the project, as well as provide transparency and insight for how well the project is tracking against financial objectives.

- Financial management approach
  - Approach for managing project costs including the estimation process, forecasting, budgeting, tracking actual costs, variance reporting and management reporting.
  - Documented calendar of financial processes, timings and frequency.
  - Alignment of project cost management approach with corporation standard approach, tools and process.
  - Alignment of financial management process to change management process, to assess impact of proposed changes on project cost.
- Estimation tools and models
  - Understand what tools and methods are used for developing project cost estimates.
  - Approach to maintain project estimation tools and assumptions based on historical actual costs.
- Cost tracking
  - Review any cost tracking models to understand how actual costs are captured and how costs are tracked at various levels (e.g. project, program, capability, cost type, etc.).

- o Confirm alignment of cost tracking tools and processes with documented corporation standards.
- o Review financial reports and variances to get a sense of how the project is tracking against budget goals.
- Reporting
  - o Understand how costs, forecasts and variances are being reported to project stakeholders including the content, timing and format.

4.4.4 Considerations

Since the size and complexity (and therefore cost) of projects continues to increase, and corporations are investing more money into their project portfolios, it is important to spend the appropriate amount of time in understanding how costs are being managed and reported on the project.

Understand corporation standards

Because financial management is an important function within corporations, and many corporations have large project investment portfolios, there are usually documented standards for how to plan, manage, track and report on project costs including tools and a specific cadence of calendared activities. These standard tools, expectations and processes for managing project costs should be understood by the assessment team, and used as a framework to compare the project against during the review.

Single source of truth for financials

Project financials should be managed in one place to ensure transparency and clarity of the numbers. This also avoids confusion if there are multiple, financial spreadsheets with different values. Most corporations have a centralized tool for managing financials, but the project may also have developed something for assessing and reporting on their specific project financial information.

Check the math

Finances are typically managed in spreadsheets many times and it is common to see math errors or mistakes in formulas (such as missing a row or column of information). These errors could result in reporting incorrect financial information which could be misleading, or even have a negative impact on the program results. The assessment team should review the financial reports for accuracy and quality.

Specifics and traceability

Projects can have many moving parts and, if possible, costs should be able to be assigned back to individual projects, deliverables and organizations. Having a granular view of project costs traced to deliverables, allows for better management of the work, an understanding of what causes are driving budget variances, and help with understanding options when cost overruns occur. The assessment should look to confirm that financials are managed at a detailed level, and investigate areas where there are large buckets of money being held without much detail, as this may indicate challenges with planning, forecasting or unallocated funds.

Alignment to change management

Cost management is tied very closely to the change management process. Once estimates are created and the budgets are set, the change management process is critical to ensure that as scope evolves and as the project progresses, any changes to the assumptions, scope, or cost get tightly managed. As changes get introduced, the team should be assessing the financial impacts of those changes so that informed decisions can be made. The same process should be followed for key decisions which have financial implications. The assessment should look for this linkage between the cost management and change management processes and the documents which support them, such as financial information on the change log.

4.4.5 Case study

The bigger the program, the bigger the problems

I was asked to take over the planning and management of an IT program which cost several hundred millions of US dollars, spanned many years, and was the largest program in the corporation that I was working for at the time. The program had been active for nearly two years and the corporation had invested millions of dollars in it already.

When I first took over the program, I performed an overall assessment of the program management structure, processes and deliverables, to understand what was in place already and where potential gaps may exist. While I had findings in several areas of the program, the financial management gaps were troubling to me, given the amount of money that the corporation was investing into the program (and had already invested in it). Some of the examples are listed below:

- The program had hundreds of employees, vendors and contractors working on it, so resources were a big part of the cost estimate, however, the resource forecasts were not accurate.

- There was no consistent approach, or model, for estimating work, effort, or resource needs on the program.

- In the prior year before I was engaged, the program was over the original budget by tens of millions of dollars.

- Financials were tracked at the individual project level but there was not much tracking at the program level.

- There was inconsistent management reporting and no detailed transparency into cost variances.

Given these identified challenges, I then spent the next few months organizing the program management office, defining the operational processes, and codifying the approach to properly manage the costs of the program.

- First, I organized the program management office around the various functions and dedicated resources to specific areas. For example, one person was responsible for program financials, one person was responsible for resource management with the corporation standard tool, another person was responsible for vendor and contract management, and one person maintained the estimation tools.

- The team then developed a playbook for the program management processes including identifying roles and responsibilities, and documenting the approach for how to manage all aspects of the program.

- We developed a consistent estimation process and tool, where the project managers facilitated input from the team members regarding the effort, duration and timing of work, along with specific resource needs which was then translated into cost based on role-specific rates.
- We created a financial calendar to show the cadence of when financial activities were due, when information would be ready to analyze, when to assess variances, and when to report findings.
- We developed a cost dashboard and tied actual costs to forecasts organized by project, organization and cost type.
- We formalized trend analysis and variance analysis for financial reporting and management updates.
- We also implemented a formal change management process to document every change, with the financial impact of that change.

The operational activities which we implemented and the number of resources in the program office seemed like they might be "overkill" but having this amount of rigor on a multi-hundred-million dollar program was needed, to ensure that we were managing the corporation's investment properly. The net result was more transparency into our financials, and for the first year after these improvements were implemented, the program came within 1% of the original budget which was more than one hundred million US dollars. Also, several of the tools and processes that we developed were leveraged by other programs within the corporation and considered best practices for their functions.

4.5 Resource management

4.5.1 Description and value

Resource management on a project refers to the planning and managing of the resources required to complete the project milestones and activities. It should be recognized that resource management is related to schedule management and financial management, as shown in *Figure 4.4*. The project schedule is the collection of activities that resources work on with their associated duration, and then the project resource cost is comprised of resource rates applied over the duration of the assignment of that resource. Therefore, while this book separates these three functions for purposes of explaining them individually, it is important to consider them as interrelated and review them as such.

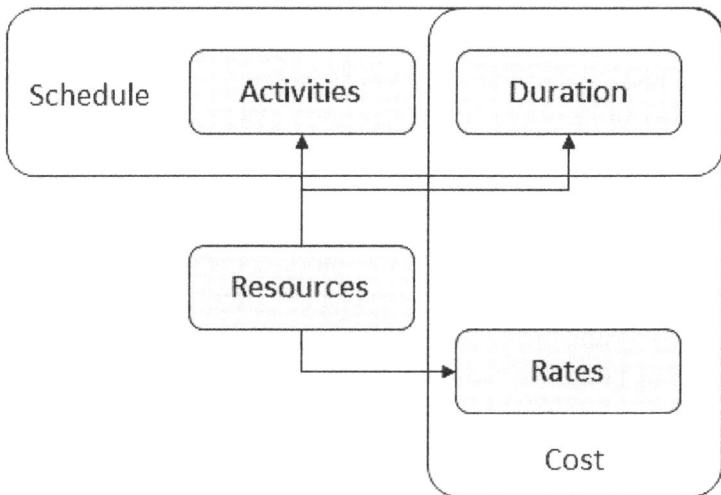

Figure 4.4: Resource management relationship

Resource management is comprised of several functions including resource planning, capacity management and resource management. Resource planning includes the identification and management of resources with the right skills required to perform the project activities. Capacity management is the alignment of the supply of these resources with the demand for those skills across a program. Lastly, resource management then involves the management of the resources as they perform the project work.

Resource planning

Resource planning occurs early in the project lifecycle and is when the project will determine what resources are required to perform the activities including the specific skills of the resources and the duration of time that the resources are required. This is also known as the resource demand.

In many corporations, projects will need to work with the internal organizations that own the resources to identify available resources with the right skills needed to perform the required work. This can be considered the supply side of resource management. Sometimes new employee hires or external contractors are needed to fill resource needs on projects. This can be in the case where specialized skills are needed and do not exist, or in the case where a certain type of resource is not available within an organization. Note that when external contractors are used on projects, there is usually a premium cost which needs to be accounted for in the project budget.

Resource planning also includes ensuring that the resources have whatever they need to perform their assigned project work which could include onboarding materials, training plans, a location to sit with the project team, and access to certain software programs. The project should have a standard approach and checklist for ensuring this.

Capacity management

Capacity management is the approach where project managers work with the resourcing organizations to align resources to the work. Many corporations manage the capacity of their resources in a human resource management system which allows for the planning of resources on projects. These systems are used to match resource supply and demand, and also involve making sure that project resources are fully allocated to work. This is important as it becomes the tool by which projects can optimize the use of resources.

Additionally, projects can use more advanced resource planning functions including resource leveling, where resources are aligned to granular tasks with effort which is then analyzed to determine how many hours of work each resource is assigned per week. The work is then "leveled" to ensure that it is evenly distributed over time. For example, a 400 hour project activity could be assigned to one person for 40 hours per week for ten weeks, or to two people for five weeks.

Resource management

Once resources are assigned to the project, there needs to be continued management of the resource information. Some of these activities are listed below:

- Management of the resource roster which could contain the full inventory of project team members, organizations, role and contact information.

- Monitoring work allocations of resources to ensure planning assumptions are correct and that team members are working the appropriate amount of time.

- Monitor start dates and end dates to ensure resources start and end on time, as there are financial implications to retaining resources longer than planned.

- Alignment of resource management to change management to assess the impact of changes on resource needs.

Resource information can be monitored and reported across all of the functions. These reports can include an identification of the program resource needs, a roster of resources with their allocations to specific program activities, and an inventory of open roles with their progress towards being filled.

In the case of programs, resource management becomes more significant than with projects because there are many more resources to plan for and manage. There are also more interdependencies of roles on programs which require diligence and transparency to avoid confusion, or gaps, in work.

Resource management is a critical function because the resources on a project are the key to its success. Projects can be considered as an aggregation of activities performed by resources to meet a common goal, so without the proper attention to the resources a project will not be successful. Mariette Keshishian and Patricia Walkow say it well when they say that "the greatest technology does not make a project successful. People do." (Keshishian and Walkow 2010). Therefore, the assessment should look at how resources are planned and managed as an indicator of future project success.

4.5.2 Key roles and focus areas

The interviews should focus on the approach for managing resources, as well as identifying any resource management risks on the project.

- PMO
  - o Discuss the approach for resource management on the project including planning of resources, capacity planning, alignment to work, and forecasting of resource needs.
  - o Review the process for defining roles and responsibilities.
  - o Review the onboarding process for new resources.
- Project manager
  - o Review the project organizational structure and associated roles and responsibilities.
  - o Identify any unfilled project roles.
  - o Discuss if there are any challenges with resource competencies or allocations to not be able to perform their work.
  - o Discuss the morale of the team to understand challenges.
  - o Understand what they are spending their time on.
- IT lead and business lead
  - o Get their perspectives on any resource challenges on the project.
- Team members
  - o Discuss if they have everything that they need to perform their project roles successfully.
  - o Confirm if roles and responsibilities are clear on the project.
  - o Discuss the morale of the team to understand challenges.

4.5.3 Key documents and focus areas

The documents reviewed should provide insight into resource roles, responsibilities, structure and planning for the project.

- Resource management approach
  - o Approach for managing resources including planning for capacity, tracking resources and onboarding.
- Project organization chart
  - o Review to see if a structure exists which includes the key roles and current content.
  - o Names should be assigned to the primary roles.
- Documented roles and responsibilities
  - o Roles should align to the project organization chart.
  - o Confirm that roles and responsibilities are documented and align with corporation standard definitions.
- Resource roster
  - o Identification of the team members with their corresponding roles on the project and organization.
  - o Confirm alignment of resources to projects with allocations by month.
  - o Confirm start and end dates for resources.
- Onboarding plan
  - o Confirm onboarding approach exists and the content is current.
- Training plan
  - o Training plan for specific skills and needs.

4.5.4 Considerations

Regarding resource management, the assessment should look at the documents and process but should also focus on the "people" side of the project to ensure that the team feels that they have what they need to be successful, and that there is the right match of need to resource skill set and dedication.

Clarity of roles

As projects grow in size, the number of different types of roles and their interdependencies continues to grow as well. It is not uncommon today for projects to have multiple types of architects, business analysts and project managers who all focus on different aspects of their domains. For example, instead of having one project architect on a project, there could be roles, such as a solution architect, performance architect, data architect, infrastructure architect and process architect.

Projects which do not have clear roles or accountabilities struggle with missed work, duplicity of work, confusion and low morale. The assessment should ensure that the roles are clearly stated in a document, and that the project team is aware, and understands them and their differences.

Having the right fit

Having the project organization structure defined, and people assigned to the specific roles, may not be sufficient if the resources are the wrong "fit" for the roles. It is not enough to just have a team member name assigned to a project role; the resources need to be capable of performing the role. The project assessment should be sensitive to this and look for areas where team members may not be performing their role optimally, and resource changes may need to be considered.

In some assessments, project sponsors may ask for the assessment to look at the competencies of the team members. The assessment team should determine the best way to review competencies and focus on specific facts, and evidence, to justify their findings. It may also make sense to work with the local human resources organization which probably has processes and thoughts around measuring competencies, especially if the results will feed into performance management processes.

Morale

Projects have many moving parts and work associated to them which require team members to be put in stressful situations which could lead to low morale.

- *Feeling overwhelmed* – projects can have busy periods of time, especially if they are behind schedule, and team members can get overwhelmed with their workload.

- *Not feeling like they are valued* – some employees could start feeling like they are not valued if they have bad experiences at work, inadequate managers, or do not feel like they are recognized for their work.

- *Not seeing action* – team members who escalate issues or decisions which do not get acted on, could start losing confidence in the project and management.

- *Interpersonal dynamics* – there can often be conflicts between team members who have different work styles, or personalities, or even have a history between each other outside of work.

- *Corporation dynamics* – corporation policies may make people nervous that they would lose their jobs in strategies, such as offshoring of work.

The impact of low morale on projects is significant and includes turnover of key resources, poor quality, and the inability to attract new resources which could all impact project goals. Morale needs to be investigated during the assessment, to determine if it exists and what the cause of it is. Note that the findings do not have to necessarily be formally documented in the assessment but would be valuable to the project leadership to understand.

Part time focus

In this world of matrixed organizations, many corporations allocate specialized resources across multiple projects. Every project manager knows that two resources allocated at 50% does not equal one full time resource. This is because there will always be conflicts with partially allocated resources, resulting in a lack of focus, missed meetings and inconsistent availability. While this may be a function of how corporations work today, the assessment team should look for cases where there are critical resources that are not fully allocated, to understand if there are impacts as a result of the part time focus.

The other type of part time focus to consider is when team members are not optimally spending their time on the right activities. Some corporations have portfolio management organizations, or framework organizations that generate a lot of paperwork. The net result is the project manager spending a lot of time on administrative activities and filling out multiple, redundant status forms. This is instead of focusing on managing their plans and driving risks, issues and decisions to closure. It may make sense for the assessment team to look into how the team members are spending their time, to see if there are opportunities to optimize it, as the following case study will demonstrate.

4.5.5 Case study

Good resource management structure but the execution was not optimal

At one corporation that I worked for, I was asked by the chief information officer to assess a two hundred million dollar program which had been underway for a little over one year. I conducted several interviews and reviewed as many program documents as I could get my hands on. Specific to resource management, the processes were solid, with detailed staffing models, organizational charts, capacity models and proper allocations of resources to activities. All of the expected resource documents and processes existed, yet when I interviewed the team members there was a common theme around the pace and complexity of the program being challenging to many of the team members.

This program had several project managers and they all discussed the challenges with the pace of the program, and their inability to stay on top of risks and issues. Therefore, I thought that it would be a good idea to assess what activities the project managers were spending their time on, and then compare that to an industry benchmark, to see if there were differences in time spent or opportunities for optimization of time. After collecting the information I found that, on average, the project managers were working 55 hour weeks, and their allocations of time are identified below.

- 31% of time on project planning
- 2% on scope management

- 2% on quality management
- 3% on issue management
- 5% on resource management
- 19% on communications management
- 12% on procurement management
- 26% on other activities including administration, filling out templates, etc.

There were a few significant findings from this review of where time was being spent. For example, according to some industry benchmarks, project managers should be spending about 15-20% of their time on issue and risk management, and here they were only spending 3% of their time. They were also spending over one quarter of their time on administrative activities not directly related to managing the project.

These insights allowed the program management team to reconsider some of the administrative activities including reducing duplicative meetings and hiring some additional program management office support resources. These changes allowed the project managers to focus more time on their plans, risks and issues which ultimately allowed the projects to be more successful.

This is a good example of an assessment that was not just focused on "checking the box" to see if resource plans existed (because in this case, they did), but then went deeper into how resources were performing their roles, and ultimately uncovered some inefficiencies which were able to be addressed.

4.6 Communication and stakeholder management

4.6.1 Description and value

Communication plays a significant role in managing projects. According to some industry estimates, a project manager spends upwards of 80% of their time involved in some form of project communications. A project manager must use several types of communication which involves constant transparency of relevant and updated project information. There are many examples of information needs and communication types for a typical project, some of which are documented below:

- *Status reports* – stakeholders need to understand the progress of a project related to its commitments. Typically, a weekly status report is generated which contains key information for stakeholders. This report can include deliverables completed and recent accomplishments, upcoming milestones, and any issues or risks that require attention, with the respective action plan. Status reports can also show a color coded "health" of the project, along areas, such as scope, resources, cost, schedule and quality.

- *Management reports* – management needs to know progress towards goals, and any escalation of issues, risks, or changes that can have an impact on the project commitments. These need to be organized and documented correctly, with a description of the challenge, impacts and alternatives, with a recommendation. Generally, management reporting is higher level than a status report, and focuses on the key milestones and major risks and issues impacting progress.

- *Stakeholder meetings* – projects (and especially programs) have many stakeholders with different agendas and interest, and therefore several meetings are often required to keep them informed, or even involve them in the management or governance process. These meetings can be used as verbal updates on the status report, or working sessions on addressing the risks and issues.

- *General communication methods* – projects can also generate newsletters, email updates, town hall meetings, or other means of keeping the teams updated on progress and key project information, as well as recognize key milestones or achievements that the team has accomplished.

- *Project documents* – projects develop many artifacts, documents and deliverables which are used at various stages of the project delivery lifecycle. Some of these documents are critical for delivering the project objectives and contain key information, such as requirements or designs.

Since there are many stakeholders on a project, it is important to identify them and develop a plan to communicate information to them, and manage their expectations around information. The project assessment should look for a thoughtful project communications plan which includes the following information:

- *Stakeholder identification* – create an inventory of the stakeholders who require communication, as well as what information they need. Stakeholders can include team members, management, other departments in the corporation, managers of project resources, and vendors. Each stakeholder may require different information so it is important to consider and document each one.

- *Communication type* – identify the type of communications which can include meetings, status reports, newsletters or emails.

- *Frequency* – determine the frequency of each communication (e.g. a weekly status report or monthly steering committee meetings).

- *Source* – identification of the source that will be used to provide the information for the communication.

- *Owner* – naming an owner from the project who will be responsible for each communication.

- *Comments* – any comments or notes which are relevant regarding the communication approach or stakeholders.

Another area of focus around the management of communications should be document management. Projects generate a considerable number of documents so it is important to store them in a single and organized location. Important documents should also be version controlled so that version history can be captured. For some documents, approvals should also be captured. The assessment should identify key documents, as well as review the process for maintaining and approving those documents.

Programs generally have more stakeholders, more scope, and more work associated with them as compared to projects. This means that communications need to account for more information and more stakeholders to satisfy. Therefore, programs should have a very well defined and managed communications approach.

4.6.2 Key roles and focus areas

Interviewing project team resources will not only confirm that the project communications plan is in place but can also validate that the communications are effective, and sufficient, for their needs.

- IT lead, business lead and sponsor
  - ○ Obtain their views on the adequacy of project communications to confirm if they are getting the information that they need, at the right time, with the right level of detail.
- Project manager
  - ○ Review the communications approach, plan and stakeholder matrix.
  - ○ Review the process for developing status reports including what information is used, the sources of that information, and how the reports get presented.
- PMO
  - ○ Discuss approach for managing project communications including identification of stakeholders, communication mechanisms and plans.
  - ○ Understand approach for maintaining, versioning, storing and approving key documents.
- Team members
  - ○ Confirm that the team members feel like they are getting relevant project information in a timely manner.

4.6.3 Key documents and focus areas

The project assessment should look for good structure around stakeholder identification and communications planning, and then assess the implementation of those plans through sample communication documents.

- Stakeholder matrix
  - ○ Identification of all project stakeholders with their respective roles.
  - ○ Understanding of what information each stakeholder needs, based on their project role.

- Communication approach and plan
  - o Documented plan for communications to different stakeholders.
  - o Plan for different types of communication formats and frequencies to various audiences (e.g. weekly status report).
  - o Plan for communicating team changes or project announcements.
  - o Approach for management of documents including folder structure and versioning.
- Project document inventory
  - o Confirm that there is a central location for storing project documents.
  - o Structure of repository is logical and organized.
  - o Look for version controls for key documents.
- Sample status report and management report
  - o Demonstrates progress updates against milestones and commitments.
  - o Transparency in risks and issues for management attention.
  - o Determine if status is driven from metrics and facts.
- Sample meeting agenda and minutes
  - o Structured agendas and meeting minutes templates.

4.6.4 Considerations

Communications management is the "glue" that keeps the project team and stakeholders informed of progress, and allows management to understand risks and issues in order to take action against them. Therefore, they should be reviewed carefully as part of the project assessment.

Program stakeholder understanding

Since there are many stakeholders on the project, it is important to identify all stakeholders and ensure that they have what they need. For example, project team members may want information on key decisions, management may want to see progress against goals, and controllers may want to see financial status. The assessment should investigate the communications plan and confirm with stakeholders that they are getting sufficient and relevant information.

Also, team members can tend to get focused on their specific activities, and then lose focus of the big picture. The project manager needs to continually communicate the vision, priorities, approach and plan to the team members, to keep them focused, and at the same time aware of the overall progress and goals. They also need to understand the day to day health of the projects and how the work they are performing is trending.

Metric based reports

Status reports can come in many different formats and structures. Generally, it is better to have metrics and milestones in the status report, as opposed to statements of progress. All milestones, issues, risks and actions in the status report should have a date associated to it, and those dates should be managed properly so that the status report always has current content. Also, as much as possible, metrics should be compared against a plan. For example, stating that ten requirement documents are complete is interesting but compared to a plan of 20, the team is behind schedule.

Structure is important

Communications and documents should be structured and well organized so that the audience can easily find them and interpret them. For example, document folders which are just large repositories of random files make it hard to find anything. Also, communications should be structured well, to tell the right story, and get the key messages across.

4.6.5 Case study

A large program with team members in the dark

During my role as an internal consultant, I conducted several project and program assessments across the corporation that I was working for. One particular program had significant challenges around communications planning and management. These challenges were mostly revealed during interviews with the program team members, who were very frustrated with the program management, lack of communications, and general confusion surrounding important information. The assessment findings regarding communications management included the following examples:

- Stakeholders were identified and documented in the program charter but there was no documented stakeholder matrix for communications.

- The program status showed some milestones and cost but they were not really tracked. For example, the financial forecast.

- There were not many documented agendas or meeting minutes and where there were minutes, they did not include specific issues, or actions, with names assigned to them or target completion dates.

- Program updates to the team were few and far between. For example, the team was not made aware one member was leaving, nor was the team made aware when new team members were joining the program.

- There was a team meeting at 8.15am every morning but it was managed "off the cuff", with no agenda. The team did not know priorities and were told information that day of the meeting, and felt like the focus for that meeting was on the "fire of the day", instead of being planned out.

- The program executives did not feel like they had enough transparency into the program. They felt like the program was having trouble but could not ascertain that from the communications and status that they had been receiving.

- Documents were not well organized on a shared folder structure, and therefore team members could not find documents that they were looking for.

Given these consistent themes from the interviews around the lack of communication planning and management, several recommendations were made to address the issues. They focused around providing more structure in planning and more transparency in the delivery of program information. The following recommendations were made and delivered with the plan, to implement in the first few months after the assessment:

- Starting with the identified stakeholders in the charter, document a stakeholder matrix which included their communications needs.

- Develop a communications plan which identified the types of communications and meetings, and included the objectives, audience and frequency.

- Update the project status report to include better structure and transparency. The proposal was to use a report that I was using on other programs which included health colors, milestones, and risks/issues with their associated action plan that included names and completion dates.

- Develop a new program folder structure based on the program organization (e.g. by program and project) and phases of the projects, and then move the files to their respective folders.

- Develop standards for communications documents which include agendas, meeting minutes and versioning.

After the assessment revealed some of the challenges, the program manager decided to leave the program (and the corporation). The new program manager came onboard and within the first two months had implemented all of the above recommendations (amongst others) which resulted in a significant improvement in transparency and clarity for the program team members, stakeholders and leadership team.

4.7 RAID management

4.7.1 Description and value

Project plans are developed to identify the key deliverables, milestones and activities performed on a project. But, as the project moves through the delivery lifecycle, there are many other real time activities which need to be managed. This includes risks and issues that arise, action items that need to be performed, and decisions that need to be made. It is important for projects to identify and manage these with the same level of rigor that is used to manage the project plan. Some projects and corporations manage these in one document, called a RAID log which is an acronym for Risks, Actions, Issues and Decisions. Many corporations have a standard for how to manage the RAID items which should be understood as part of planning for the project assessment.

Risk management

Risk management is the identification, assessment, and prioritization of risks, followed by the coordinated and economical application of resources to minimize, monitor, and control the probability and/or impact of unfortunate events (Hubbard 2009). Projects inherently have risks associated with them, and as projects and their solutions get larger and more complex, so do the risks and their implications. Therefore, risk management is a critical part of project management and has to be embedded within every aspect of project management because risks can occur anywhere.

Projects should define the approach for how to identify, track and manage risks. There are four primary steps in the risk management process:

1. *Identify risks* – the first step is identifying and documenting the risks on the project in a risk log. This requires performing regular assessments of the project, and constant monitoring of project information to identify possible risks. For example, monitoring the schedule for risks to slippage of milestones.

2. *Assess risks* – once risks are identified, they need to be assessed for impact and probability of occurrence. There are several methodologies to do this which include

weighting the risk, scoring them, or even quantifying the financial impacts of them. There also needs to be analysis of root cause, to see what is causing the risk. Once the risks are assessed, the project team needs to determine what to do with the risk and can then take the appropriate action to manage it.

3. *Take action* – upon assessment and determination of approach, the project team then needs to act on the risk. This can include accepting the risk, looking to avoid the risk, or taking specific action to reduce, or mitigate, the risk.

4. *Monitor* – risk management is a living process and therefore even if an action is already being taken, the project team must continue to monitor it to ensure that it is having the desired impact on the risk. Also, constant monitoring is important to identify additional risks, as there are always new ones popping up.

The assessment team should look for a documented risk management approach, and then review how well it is being followed on the project, for identifying and managing risks. Often, risks get recognized early on in the project but are then not maintained, or updated, as they evolve and new risks get identified.

Issue management

When project risks get realized, then they become issues. Project managers may have proper planning and diligence, resulting in the perfect schedule and estimates but if issues are not managed well, then the project will have a limited ability to be successful because they will always be "fighting fires" and reacting to issues.

Similar to risk management, the issue management process should be well documented on the project. The issue management process is also comprised of four steps.

1. *Identify issue* – when an issue is identified that usually means that there is an impact on the project which could include implications on scope, resources, financials or schedule. An issue log should be used to capture the risk information.

2. *Assess issue* – as issues arise they need to be assessed for complete impact, as well as to identify options to resolve the issue. This assessment can involve multiple project team members who have insight into the impacts of the issue, and who can offer solutions for resolving it.

3. *Escalate issue* – depending on the impact of the issue, an escalation path should be defined and used to make management aware, and facilitate any decisions needed to take action to resolve the issue. This escalation path should be documented and shared with the team for clarity of expectations.

4. *Address issue* – after action is determined, the issue needs to be aggressively managed and closed.

The project assessment team should pay close attention to how well issues are documented, how well they get escalated to management, and the speed at which they get resolved properly. Lingering issues can have significant impacts to project schedules, cost, morale and ability to meet commitments.

Action item management

The key project's activities and deliverables should be tracked within the project plan but there are also many other tasks that go beyond the planned activities which need to be tracked. These additional tasks could include preparing for important upcoming meetings, acquiring specific resources, or simply the takeaways from project team meetings. All of these tasks need to be tracked and managed, and are done so through the action item management process. There are three high level steps in this process:

1. *Identify actions* – first, the actions that need to be tracked need to be identified. Actions can arise from meetings where follow ups are identified, and should be managed in a central location.

2. *Take action* – once it is identified that action is needed, the specific next steps need to be determined and tracked. A central action item log can be used to document the action items, owners for the action, due dates and track progress.

3. *Follow up* – lastly, after the actions are completed, there should be a follow up to confirm completion, or any additional actions that may be needed. Some action items will only require being checked off when they have been completed, whereas other action items may be recurring, or may require additional follow up.

Actions arise from many different sources, and the assessment should review how well they get captured, managed and followed up on. Without proper tracking, there will be many "loose ends" on the project, and some may get lost which could have impacts on the success of the project.

Decision management

Lastly, as projects progress through their delivery lifecycle, they come to critical junctures where key decisions need to be made. Similar to risks, issues, and actions, these need to be tracked and managed on the project. The primary steps in the decision management process are outlined below:

1. *Define problem* – this first step is the identification of the problem which needs a management decision and the outcome which is desired. It is important to isolate the problem so that there is clarification around what decision is specifically required and the impacts of not making the decision.
2. *Develop options* – once a problem is identified, then information related to the problem needs to be gathered so that options can be formulated. An option can also include not taking action.
3. *Evaluate options* – the options need to be evaluated in regard to how well they solve the problem, as well as any consequences of implementing the option. A set of criteria should be considered when evaluating an option. This will be the insight used by management to make the decision, so it should be as factual and thorough as possible.
4. *Make decision* – after the options have been considered according to relevance, impact and consequences, the decision maker will make their choice. A decision log is a useful tool to document key decisions and relevant information, such as the person who made the decision, the date that the decision was made, what the decision was, and what the reasoning was for the decision.

The RAID documents are important as they represent the outstanding items on the project which need to be managed to keep work moving forward and remove obstacles that are blocking the project. The assessment should review each RAID area to understand the approach for the project, and then determine how well the approach is being followed in the management and tracking of each of the RAID items.

4.7.2 Key roles and focus areas

The interviews should focus on how the RAID inventories are used on the project, and if team members are feeling like RAID items get resolved quickly, as well as if leaders are feeling like they have transparency into RAID items properly.

- IT lead and business lead
  - o Discuss how they feel about risk, issue and decision management, and confirm that they have enough transparency into risks and issues.
  - o Discuss if they feel that issues, risks and decisions get escalated to them in a timely manner.
- PMO
  - o Review the approach for capturing and managing risks, issues, action items and decisions.
  - o Discuss the forums for reviewing and following up on these items.
- Project manager
  - o Review how they use the RAID tools to manage the program including meetings, how items get followed up on, and tracking items.
  - o Discuss how risks and issues get escalated to them and to project leadership, and any challenges they have with that process.
  - o Discuss how key decisions get identified and made, and any challenges they have.
- Team members
  - o Determine if they feel that risks and issues get escalated properly and addressed quickly.

○ Discuss how they feel about decisions being made in a timely manner.
○ Discuss how they feel about action items being identified and tracked.

4.7.3 Key documents and focus areas

The assessment should review the approach documents for each of the RAID elements, as well as review the project inventories, to see how they are being used to track and manage the RAID items.

- Risk management approach
  ○ Documented approach including identification of risks, weighting of risks and assigning actions.
- Issue management approach
  ○ Documented approach for issue identification and analysis, escalation and resolution.
- Action item management approach
  ○ Documented approach for identifying, tracking and following up on project action items.
- Decision management approach
  ○ Documented approach for making project decisions and tracking decision information.
- Risk log
  ○ Risks are identified, managed and tracked in a central risk log.
  ○ Confirm that specific actions are identified, with owners and dates for each risk in the log.
  ○ The risk log is properly maintained without many open action items past due dates.
- Issue log
  ○ Issues are managed and tracked in a central issue log.

- o Confirm that actions are identified, with owners and dates for each issue.
  - o The issue log is properly maintained without many open action items past due dates.
- Action item log
  - o Actions are managed and tracked in a central action item log.
  - o Confirm that actions are identified, with owners and target closure dates for each action.
  - o The action item log is properly maintained without many open items past due dates.
- Decision log
  - o Decisions tracked in a central location which includes information on the decision, who made it, and when it was made.

4.7.4 Considerations

There are several concepts to keep in mind when reviewing project RAID documents during the assessment.

These are living documents

Each of the RAID inventories should be considered "living", in that they get maintained and updated frequently, with relevant and timely content. These are not one-time activities and should be considered part of the day to day management of the project. There should also be a regular cadence on the project to update these items (such as during a team meeting) and then to publish them to the team in a status report.

The assessment should look to ensure that these documents are reviewed, maintained and updated frequently, as well as communicated to the project stakeholders. This includes ensuring that dates and names get assigned to each item on the inventory, and that they get managed to closure.

Use documents for management updates

Since these are the documents which highlight challenges for the project (e.g. risks, open issues, and decisions that need to be made), the assessment should confirm that the more impactful items also appear on status reports and management updates. As stated in the prior section, there should be a recurring process to identify them, update them, and report on them, so that this becomes part of the cycle of managing work, as opposed to a separate process of management escalation.

Inventories should be easily accessed

The RAID documents should be stored in a central location that the team has access to, so that they can be found, reviewed and updated easily by the project team. These documents are key parts of how the project gets managed, so they should be located in a visible place so the entire team knows where to go to view or update them.

Method for following up

Since the RAID documents should be updated frequently, the project assessment should look for the cadence of maintaining the actions and dates. This can include using regular meetings to review them, a weekly follow up by the project manager, or assigning a team member to track them down. In most cases, just having these items documented on a list is not sufficient, and they will require proactive management to bring them to closure, since team members are usually overloaded with many concurrent activities.

Think through implications

The RAID logs should be more than just inventories of risk, issue, action and decision descriptions. Ample thought needs to be put into the implications of those risks, issues and decisions. Since projects are becoming more complex, the implications of RAID items becomes more intricate and impactful if they get realized (e.g. risks and issues), or if they don't get performed (e.g. a decision is not made, or a risk is not acted on). The project team should be using architecture diagrams, technical team members, and business experts, to review and assess the impacts of these items, and the possible actions to close them so that informed steps can be taken to close them.

4.7.5 Case study

Not managing issues and risks was causing issues and risks

This case study is from the same program which I reviewed in the "Project Structure and Governance" chapter, where I was asked by the CTO to assess a $16 million program which was having problems. Consistent with the findings around the program structure, there was also a lack of structure and diligence around the management of the RAID items. There was also a feeling from the IT lead and sponsor that there was not enough transparency of the risks and issues. They felt that the program was in trouble but the program documents and weekly status reports did not corroborate their feelings, or provide them enough insight into the program challenges.

The program assessment looked at program documents and interviewed many team members who provided consistent feedback around how poorly the RAID items were managed. Some of the findings are documented below:

- Some risks were captured in program documents but did not have mitigating actions identified or owners assigned to them.

- There was a program risk log but it was very light on content and was not stored in a shared location so, when interviewed, the team members stated that they were not aware that it even existed.

- There was a program issues log but more than half of the identified issues did not have actions or dates assigned to them, and therefore they were not managed to closure in a timely manner.

- Some issues that were documented on the status report had been open for three or four months without resolution.

- Several team members stated during the interviews that they felt that issues were not being addressed. One team member was told that the IT lead had "other issues and doesn't need to be bothered with this." Another team member said that issues were not escalated until "the pressure was on." A third team member felt that when he raised issues, nothing was done with them.

- There was no decision log documented and interviews revealed that the team felt that decisions were made by committee with no one accountable, and that many decisions were not made.

As stated in the first case study, as a result of the program assessment I was asked to take over this program, restructure it, and deliver on its stated objectives. Based on the findings, I dedicated the first few weeks of my tenure on the program to collecting information so that we had a complete list of all known risks, issues and pending decisions. We created central repositories for each of the RAID items and stored them in a common location for the team to be able to find and access.

We consolidated every documented risk, issue and decision in these logs. I also met with each of the project team leads and facilitated the open items that they were aware of. We collected more than 40 outstanding risks, issues and decisions which needed to be addressed. Following this we prioritized them, discussed them and assigned names and dates to each of them. We then set up a cadence to review the progress against each of them several times per week, until the list became more manageable. It took about six weeks (which was much longer than I had expected) but we were able to close out almost all of the issues, assign actions to all of the risks, and close out many open decisions. We then set up a regular cadence to identify, discuss and manage the RAID items on a going forward basis which included understanding any new items as they arose on the program.

Finally, we aligned these RAID items with the program status report for transparency of the major risks and issues which we could discuss as we met with the leads and sponsor of the program. Between providing the structure and generating visibility of the RAID items, the program team was able to focus on taking action to address them, and ultimately improve the success of the program.

4.8 Vendor management

4.8.1 Description and value

As business processes and technology solutions become more complex and specialized, the use of vendors has been increasing on projects. With regard to information technology projects, a vendor is an organization that offers contingent labor, specialized skills or products. There are several capacities that a project may use vendors for which are outlined below. These can be used on projects and programs but are more prevalent on programs given their size, span of focus and complexity.

- *Experience* – vendors may be used for their experience in managing large and complex programs, managing initiatives similar to the one they are brought in for, or with specific technologies, solutions or products.

- *Additional resource capacity* – vendors can help with resource capacity by providing supplemental resources as projects identify additional needs which cannot be satisfied internally by the organization. This approach reduces the time it takes to recruit, hire and bring on new resources. This approach also saves the overhead cost and time of hiring resources, as well as reducing the risk of downsizing resources when programs finish and there may not be additional work. Lastly, it avoids costs for corporations, such as benefits, bonuses and training.

- *Risk sharing* – because projects are becoming more complex and risky, partnering with a vendor can help to share in the execution risk of the project which could provide a higher probability of success.

- *Specialized skills* – vendors may have expertise in specific skills where most corporations do not have resources with those set of skills. This may include new technologies, such as mobile applications, or recent trends in software development techniques, such as Agile programming.

- *Cost advantage* – many vendors offer an "offshore" model where they have resources who work on certain project roles, for lower wages, in a foreign country. The most common example of this is offshore technology programmers, who cost around half of the cost of local resources and work from India, Asia or South America. As spending on technology projects becomes more expensive to deliver, corporations are continuing to look for ways to keep technology development costs down and offshore vendors provide an opportunity to do this.

- *Product offering* – some vendors also offer technology products, or tools, which can speed up the delivery of solutions on programs. Along with purchasing the product, corporations can use professional services from these corporations to help set up, configure and implement the products as well.

Some projects use vendors as subcontractors filling specific roles, some use them as partners to deliver a specific component, and some use them as strategic delivery partners. The project assessment should seek to understand how vendors are being used, in what roles and functions they are performing, and how the working relationships with the vendors are. The assessment should also look into the approach for managing vendor information, such as contracts, invoices and payments.

4.8.2 Key roles and focus areas

Since vendors are an integral part of projects, the interviews should be focused on how well the vendors are working with the project teams, and identify any challenges that may exist with the vendors.

- IT lead
  - o Understand the strategy for the project around using vendors and in what expected capacities.
- Project manager
  - o Understand how the project uses vendors and in what capacities.
  - o Discuss how the vendor relationship is managed.
  - o Discuss how the contract was set up, including quality reviews and performance metrics.
  - o Discuss how well the partnerships are working with the vendors.
- PMO
  - o Discuss the approach for managing vendors, contracts and invoices.
- Team members
  - o Discuss how well vendors are being used on the project and any challenges that the team is having with them.
- Vendors
  - o If there are strategic partners, or vendors, in certain roles on the project, they should be considered for interviews, to get their perspective on the project and its risks, as they have outside experiences and insights which may be valuable.
  - o Vendors should be asked the interview questions for their respective roles on the project.

4.8.3 Key documents and focus areas

Most corporations have existing vendor and procurement practices which should be understood, and the project assessment should look at how the project approaches are documented and followed.

- Vendor management approach
  - Approach for vendors documented including when to use vendors, approach for procuring vendors and tracking methods.
  - Approach for managing the contracts, invoices and finances of vendors.
  - Approach for reporting on vendor resources, spend, progress against contractual milestones and risks.
- Vendor inventory
  - For larger programs with many vendors there may need to be an inventory of all vendors with associated contract, resource and schedule information.
- Vendor document repository
  - Review the location for vendor contracts and invoices. Note that these may need to be secured if sensitive financial or contractual information is included.
- Vendor scorecard
  - Some corporations require vendor scorecards, so the assessment may want to review these for insights into the vendor relationship.

4.8.4 Considerations

Increasingly, vendors are becoming an important part of the planning and execution on projects so they need to be evaluated as part of the project assessment, to have a complete picture of the project health.

Cultural fit

Vendors may work at a corporation with a different corporate culture than the corporation which owns the project being worked on. Cultural differences should be recognized and identified as they may have an impact on the project. For example, a vendor may use different tools or methods for managing project work which may be incongruent to how the project is managing them.

Many vendors leverage resources from all around the planet, so there are also geographical cultural differences which need to be recognized as well. For example, some Indian and Asian cultures can be passive and therefore possibly not raise issues immediately. Not recognizing this could impact projects if issues are not raised in a timely manner because of a cultural characteristic.

The assessment should try to identify the corporate and geographical cultural differences and highlight them as areas of focus. They should also be on the lookout for areas where these differences have had impact and note them.

Be sensitive to corporation vendor strategies

As part of a corporate strategy in some corporations, vendors were hired and brought in to replace internal resources at cheaper rates. This dynamic should be recognized prior to the project assessment, so that there is a consideration for team member reactions or lowered morale regarding the vendors on the project and fear of losing their jobs. While these are decisions made by corporation management, they may still have an impact on the performance of the project team and should be highlighted.

Monitor vendor performance

Because vendors are contractually obligated to perform work, there needs to be a level of transparency into their progress. The most common way of doing this is to set up the contract to pay based on interim milestones, and then have team members perform reviews of that work to confirm that it meets quality and contractual expectations. The project assessment should assess if these milestones are tracked and reported in the same way as the schedule is tracked for the project.

The project should also monitor vendor quality of deliverables which could include reviews and sign offs of deliverables. The contract should be set up in such a way that the project team can assess the quality of work and determine if it is acceptable before payments are made. Vendor quality should be a focus area to review.

Leverage their insight

Many vendor corporations are specialized in their areas and are recognized industry leaders. This could include being certified with accreditations that demonstrate their effectiveness. For example, many IT development organizations are certified as CMMI level 5 which means they have a highly effective delivery process.

Since these corporations are recognized as industry leaders, the project assessment should look at how the project is leveraging their expertise and talent. In some cases resources are told to perform a very specific role and not question the corporation process or framework. The assessment may also want to identify areas where the vendor is performing industry leading work and see if there are opportunities to leverage that beyond just the project being assessed. For example, some processes, tools or documents could be used to augment the corporation standard framework.

4.8.5 Case study

Strategic vendor partnership not being optimized

As stated in a prior case study, I was running the IT CMMI organization for a Fortune 100 corporation which included conducting standard program quality assessments at key points during the project lifecycle. In this case, we were asked to conduct a quality review of a multi-year and multi-million dollar initiative which was the program that was meant to enable a growing business segment to realize its strategic objectives. This program was partnering with a large consulting corporation to be a strategic delivery partner, helping to plan and execute on this program to meet its objectives.

The program was set up in a joint management approach which had co-leads from each corporation in critical program leadership roles. Some of the capability delivery was also given to the vendor to manage and deliver.

During the team member interviews, several themes emerged around the challenges of the vendor partnership and the "mixed" approach to managing and staffing the teams on the program.

- The team had been established and formed very rapidly which did not permit time for collaboration or any kind of team building, so the trust and teamwork between resources was lacking.

- There was a lack of clear roles between two corporations with leads from both corporations trying to drive work and develop program structures.

- It was unclear how much program work would be sourced to the vendor which caused confusions on roles. This was a consistent theme and also made people worried because on top of this being a complex program, they were worried about losing their jobs to the vendor as well.

- The program cost was also over budget and there was a premium cost associated with the vendor resources, so there was also confusion as to the priority of program spend and how many vendor resources would be engaged.

The assessment team worked with the program management team to determine several recommendations which would bolster the collaboration between the organizations and provide the role clarity that the team was looking for.

- Working sessions were held with the team to determine which roles would be filled with vendors and which would be internal resources. The team worked to determine the optimal consultant and employee mix for key roles, such as the PMO, program leads, business analysts, system developers and testers.

- An updated roles and responsibility matrix was created based on the solidified program structure which clarified the differences in roles between the team members and the partner resources.

- The program management office was also developed as a joint organization to manage the operations of the program, with clear accountabilities of each role within that team.

- Based on the agreed plan, vendor roles and cost were then factored into the program budget appropriately.

This program had a significant amount of work to do and it was essential to determine clarity of the vendor and employee roles so that the team would be optimized to deliver on its commitments. The team rallied around defining these roles and updated the relevant program documents which provided this clarity. Several months later, the organization did a subsequent review and, this time, the feedback from the team members was much more positive towards the joint relationship with the vendor.

4.9 Software lifecycle delivery management

4.9.1 Description and value

The premise of this book is that assessments should focus on the project management functions as the primary driver of success on projects, including influencing the delivery stages of work. However, it is also important to contemplate the project delivery lifecycle as well, since this is the primary work that will be performed on the project. *Figure 4.5* shows the typical model for software delivery.

Figure 4.5: Typical software delivery lifecycle

The standard software delivery model has six primary phases. Note that other application development models, such as iterative development or agile development, still have some form of each of these phases, even if they are not sequential as *Figure 4.5* represents. Each of these phases has specific functions, documents, roles and processes which are important to the successful delivery of the project. The following text outlines some of the key points for each of the phases.

Planning

The first phase is during the initial scoping and planning of the project which can include developing the project charter, creating the estimates, documenting the team structure and building the project plan. These areas are important to assess as they set the foundation for the project and the structure for delivering on the project goals. Note that most of the deliverables in this phase are contemplated in the project management functions in the prior sections of this chapter.

Requirements

The requirements phase documents the project objectives and scope into defined and specific functions for system delivery. This is usually performed by business analysts facilitating requirements from subject matter experts on the business teams. It is important to ensure that all requirements get documented properly, as these become the book of record for what should be developed on the project. Any requirements that are missed, or incorrectly documented, could have significant impacts on the project in terms of missed functionality, rework, additional cost and schedule slippage.

Another area to contemplate in the assessment is the traceability of the requirements through the delivery lifecycle. Since the requirement documents represent the full scope for the project, it becomes important to trace them from the beginning of the project through to development and testing, to ensure that they get delivered.

Design

During the design phase, the project team describes how desired system features will function in detail, including screen layouts, business rules, system interface information, process diagrams and other documentation. This work is typically performed by designers, or project architects, who have specialized skills in taking requirements and turning them into designs and system specifications.

The project assessment should look into any risk areas of the design which could include complex integration points, new technology products, or solutions or challenges with vendor solutions or resources. Other areas of the design that should be considered are around the technology solution and how well it is designed which could include the ability to scale, performance risks and maintainability.

Build

During the build phase, the system code is developed per the requirements and design specifications. This is where the project moves from documentation into creating working systems, developing integration points and building out interfaces. This phase also includes performing an initial unit test, by the developers, to confirm that the code is working as they expect, before moving into the more formal testing phases.

Test

The test phase consists of several types of tests which are all intended to ensure that the development meets the documented requirements and expected quality. The tests can include types such as system testing application code, integration testing of multiple components, performance testing to ensure the code will handle expected volumes, and user testing to gather user feedback.

The assessment should review the strategy and plans for testing, as there are many important activities which need to be planned out before the tests can occur including determining the types of tests to conduct, the identification of test cases, tools used, metrics and reporting. The assessment should then also analyze the execution against those plans, with proper metrics and reporting to project management.

Deploy

The deploy phase consists of the releasing of the code into the production environment where it is "live" for users. There is usually planning required to ensure that the organization is ready for the deployment which is managed under an "operational readiness" plan. This plan includes several readiness activities including release plans, contingency plans, organizational readiness plans, support processes for help desk and incident management, warranty plans, and confirming that IT controls are in place.

The project assessment should contemplate the operational readiness plans to understand how the project is preparing for the implementation of the project scope. Some of these planning activities can be split between business readiness and IT readiness so, depending on the scope of the assessment and how the project defines and organizes the work, the review should consider both areas.

4.9.2 Key roles and focus areas

There are several different roles that have specific activities on a typical technology project. The primary roles on the project team could be interviewed to gain insights into how the project is progressing towards its goals, and to understand any risks that they are aware of. In prior sections, these project roles were all grouped under the title of "team members", to get their insights into the project management functions, and therefore the areas noted below are specific to their individual roles.

- Project manager (all phases)
  - Understand their perspectives on where there may be resource or delivery risks with respect to the SDLC activities.

- PMO (all phases)
  - Review the key software delivery lifecycle processes, gates and approach for the project.

- Business analyst (requirements)
  - Review the approach for facilitating and documenting the business requirements.
  - Discuss their perspectives on the risks, or challenges, with collecting business requirements.

- Subject matter expert (requirements)
  - Discuss their perspectives on the risks, or challenges, with documenting business requirements.

- Architect/designer (design)
  - Review the approach for translating the requirements into designs and system specifications.
  - Discuss the approach for the solution including integration points, maintainability, scalability and performance.

o Discuss their perspectives on the risks, or challenges, with designing the system solutions.

- Developer (build)
  o Discuss their perspectives on the risks, or challenges, with developing and testing application code including fixing identified defects.

- Test planner (test)
  o Review the approach for the test strategy, or plans, including approach for testing, metrics, defect management, reporting, data, and environments.
  o Discuss their perspectives on the risks, or challenges, with test planning.

- Tester (test)
  o Discuss their perspectives on the risks, or challenges, with test execution.

- Operational readiness PM (deploy)
  o Discuss the approach for preparing the organization for the deployment of the project scope including contingency planning, release planning, training, and any warranty support or command center strategies.
  o Discuss the approach for updating operational support processes, such as incident management, change management and help desk procedures.
  o Review the key deployment risks for the project.

- Vendors
  o Discuss any challenges, or risks, that the vendors observe with the specific phases or roles within the project lifecycle.

4.9.3 Key documents and focus areas

There are key documents which are produced specific to each SDLC phase. Depending on the scope and objectives of the project assessment, the assessment team may want to review some of these documents. Note that the key documents from the Planning phase have already been identified in earlier chapters, such as the project charter and plan.

- SDLC (all phases)
  - Standard methodology is documented and being used on the project.
  - Roles and responsibilities should be documented for SDLC artifacts.
- Requirements documents (requirements)
  - Requirements management including the collection of requirements, what tools to use, the sign off process, and traceability.
  - Documented business and functional requirements which may include process flows, data, and other technical requirements (e.g. performance and security).
  - Requirement documents should have reviews and sign offs.
- Design documents (design)
  - Approach for documenting designs, confirming that designs meet requirements and sign offs.
  - Review the design documents to see how the approach was used.
  - Documented approach for nonfunctional requirements, such as scalability, maintainability, security and performance.
- Build and unit test (build)
  - Code delivery.

o Confirm that unit test results are documented and demonstrate ample testing and defect resolution.

- Test planning (test)
  o Test approach and strategy document; a comprehensive approach for all types of testing including data, environments, tools, the defect management process and metrics for reporting.
  o Test plans should follow the test strategy and approach.

- Test execution (test)
  o Test results confirm that testing was completed per the plan.
  o Reports and metrics should exist for transparency of testing progress.

- Operational readiness plans (deploy)
  o Approach for operational readiness which includes planning for releases, contingency planning, training and organizational readiness.
  o Documented release and contingency plans for project releases.
  o Approach for documenting and tracking technology controls.
  o Documented changes to operational processes, such as incident management, change management and service management.
  o Project closure documents to track lessons learned.

4.9.4 Considerations

Projects follow a delivery lifecycle and challenges can arise at any point during the process and therefore the assessment should evaluate the entire lifecycle, looking for areas of risk or challenges.

Reviews and sign offs

Many application delivery frameworks identify reviews and sign offs as documented steps, but that does not mean that every project uses them. Often, projects will have schedule constraints and move past these steps in order to move forward. This can cause problems later because, without proper reviews and sign offs, the project can have reword, missed requirements or misinterpreted requirements. The project assessment should pay particular attention to the approach for conducting reviews and obtaining sign offs of key documents, and then examine the documents to see if it was followed, as well as inquire about this during the team member interviews.

Consider scenarios and end to end flows

Projects can have a significant amount of requirements, interface points and complexity. Projects should consider creating scenarios, such as use cases for requirements or end to end process flows which can identify these scenarios, which will then translate into design flows and testing scenarios. Just having a static inventory of requirements may not be sufficient to cover all scenarios that the business is expecting, which could lead to gaps in functionality or expected outcomes.

The assessment should look to see how requirements, design and testing are completed with end to end flows or scenarios and, if they are not, the assessment team should investigate how these are considered, or if there are gaps that need to be addressed.

Look for the handoffs

The IT delivery lifecycle is made up of specific phases of work and specialized resources so there are many handoffs between team members and project roles. For example, the business analyst hands off the business requirements to the designer who, in turn, hands off the solution design documents to the developers, who hand off completed code to the testers. During these handoffs, there is the risk of misinterpreting information, or possible oversights of important content. The project assessment should investigate how the handoffs are conducted and look for opportunities to ensure that the proper knowledge is transitioned from one team to the next on the project.

Specialized assessment topics

Beyond reviewing the software delivery lifecycle documents and approach, there can also be specialized topics that get requested for review, such as Sarbanes Oxley financial processes, application security protocols, or financial controls. These are usually performed by trained internal audit staff. The assessment should understand upfront their scope of work with respect to these items, and the expectations of the project assessment.

Mixed delivery methodologies

This chapter focused on a more standard (or "waterfall") approach of IT delivery but there are others types of delivery that can get used. Projects that contain components which are delivered using different methodologies, have their own set of challenges around the interactions between the different models. If the project being assessed has this scenario, the assessment team may want to investigate how well the methodologies are integrating on the project, and identify any possible risks or known challenges.

4.9.5 Case study

Performing an end to end quality assessment

I was asked by the Chief Information Office of a business segment to conduct a project quality review for a mid-sized program within one of the business segments. This request meant a complete assessment of the program which was early in the build phase at the time of the assessment. This program was implementing a packaged product with existing systems to enhance business capabilities for the customers of the corporation, so it had internal and external visibility.

The corporation had a standard project quality review checklist and set of focus areas, so that was used as a foundation for the approach, scope and plan for the assessment. After several weeks of collecting information, several key findings were documented which spanned the delivery lifecycle.

- **Requirements**
  - o While requirement documents existed, end to end business process flows were not documented.
  - o There was no detailed traceability of scope from requirement documents through to testing documents.
  - o Requirements were documented in several places and there was no central requirements inventory.
  - o The nonfunctional requirements were not captured in any documents (e.g. security and performance)
- **Design and build**
  - o There were concerns with the performance of the solution and product which needed to be tested.
  - o The plan did not account for upgrades to the primary product which was being used for the solution.

- o There were identified gaps with the infrastructure environment needed for testing and deploying the solution.
- **Test**
  - o Some testing processes were documented but not all were defined in the approach, or were clear to the program team.
  - o There was a tool used as the primary source of defect tracking but the vendor could not access it.
  - o The testing plans were not fully developed including several functions and areas not having plans at all.
  - o The approach for traceability of test cases back to scope and requirements was not clearly documented.
  - o The team has some automated test scripts but they were not being updated as changes were made, so they were not very useful for the team.
- **Deploy**
  - o The release plan was not fully documented.
  - o The approach for preparing the organization for the new system and functionality was not documented.

The team then proposed specific recommendations for each of the identified challenges. This included cleaning up the requirement and design documents, developing better infrastructure and performance plans, and focusing on improvements in test planning. Since the assessment was conducted during the build phase, the project had time to implement these recommendations and yield the benefits before the end of the program.

CHAPTER 5: ASSESS AND RECOMMEND

Once the project information is gathered, it needs to be reviewed and assessed to pull out relevant content, observations and insights. This information will then be used to document the project assessment findings, determine a set of recommendations to optimize the project delivery, and take action on the risks and challenges. This chapter will explore some methods for assessing the project information, identify some key items to look for, and review the approach for determining a set of recommendations.

5.1 Assessment framework

The "art" of the project assessment is taking all of the disparate information gathered from interviews, document reviews and observations, and then synthesizing it into relevant findings. This is where the experience of the assessment team becomes important but there are a few different methods that could be used for assessing the information. These are highlighted in *Table 5.1*, along with some suggestions on when to use each method, as well as some "pros" and "cons" of each.

Table 5.1: Assessment approach comparison

Approach	When to Use	Pros	Cons
Framework Compliance	Goal is to confirm the use of corporation standard documents	• Can use an existing framework as a starting point	• Does not focus on how project is being managed • Does not focus on the team dynamics
Inventory and Organize Risks	Goal is to have a complete picture of project risks	• Full view of all project risks • Allows for team perceptions	• Findings are not quantified or measured, so hard to see relative impact and priority
Scoring	Goal is to highlight relative risk areas or measure adequacy against a rating scale	• Shows health relative to a scale • Easy high level view of health factors	• May be hard to measure and quantify some risks
Benchmark Compare	Goal is to determine how project is being managed as compared to industry benchmarks	• Uses industry measurements and best practices • Adds credibility	• May be hard to normalize project data with industry data and compare them

Compliance to a corporation standard framework

The most basic way to assess project information would be to start with a checklist from a corporation framework and review whether or not the project has created all of the relevant project documentation. Many corporations have a standard set of project deliverables and processes which are expected to be completed for each phase, such as the project charter during the planning phase, or use cases during the requirements phase.

This list of mandatory documents can be used to set expectations for projects including what deliverables should be in their plans, and what they will be assessed for during quality reviews or phase gate meetings. The assessment can then review each item in the checklist and identify gaps between the checklist and the project documentation.

This approach can determine if key project documents exist, but often does not get very detailed information on how the documents are used, or how well the project is being managed. The approach also does not provide the perspectives, observations and concerns from the project team members. For these reasons it could be good to assess framework compliance but it may not be a very effective approach for improving the probability of project success.

Inventory and organize the risks

During the information collection phase of the assessment, many risks and challenges get identified. The assessment team may want to capture and build an inventory of the identified risks, and then review them for similarities which could allow them to be grouped together into categories. For example, the risks could be organized by the project phase (e.g. requirements or testing), or by the project management area (e.g. scope management or schedule management). This approach enables the insights from the team members to be organized, along with the documentation findings, into logical categories of work.

This approach is useful for organizing the content and seeing the breadth of challenges on the project. The assessment team should look to identify the impacts of these risks beyond just collecting them. For example, if there are risks with delays in the project schedule, then the impact may be a delay in the overall project timeline, or a reduction in the realization of business benefits.

This approach is good at aggregating the project risks but is not very quantitative. Just collecting and documenting the risks does not let stakeholders understand the magnitude of the risks, or the relative priority and impact between them. This is a good starting point but the assessment could be more effective (and valuable) by looking into scoring or benchmarks.

Scoring framework

Another assessment approach is to use a framework to "score" risk categories or project areas. In this model, each category gets a score based on a defined set of criteria and the findings of the assessment. The areas which can be scored include the project management functions (e.g. schedule, resources and cost), project phases (e.g. requirements, build and test), or other defined project dimensions.

There are several different models which can be used to score the project assessment findings. Three of these include a relative scoring model, a numbering scale model, and a graphical display model.

1. *Relative scoring* – in this assessment model a score is assigned to each category relative to each other, based on a defined criteria set. For example, the scale could be impact of risk and the ratings could be "high", "medium" and "low." *Figure 5.1* shows a scale of function adequacy where the relative scores include "adequate", "identified opportunities or risks" and "needs improvement." In this example, the project scope management was found to be adequate, whereas the cost management function needs improvement, and the other areas have some risks identified. There is also a high level description for each function which justifies the score for that function.

Project Function	Score	Score Justification
Schedule Management	⊕	Schedule missing critical path and dependencies
Scope Management	●	Scope well defined
Resource Management	⊕	Not all key roles filled
Cost Management	○	Financial tracking has deficiencies

● Adequate   ⊕ Opportunities/Risks   ○ Needs Improvement

Figure 5.1: Relative score model

2. *Numbering scale* – another assessment model uses numbers to score each component, based on a defined scale. This approach can also color code the scores based on the numbers, which is otherwise known as a "heat map" of colors, going from green (best score) to red (worst score). *Figure 5.2* demonstrates an example where the numbering scale is measuring how well defined each of the key project management deliverables are on a particular project, with the lowest number being the best score and the highest number

being the worst. In this case, the project charter exists and is current (score of 1) but the communication plan does not exist (score of 5).

Category	Rating
Project Charter	1
Project Plan	2
Resource Plan	3
Budget	2
RAID Log	4
Communication Plan	5

Legend
1. Exists and updated
2. Exists but needs to be updated
3. Contains most key elements
4. Missing many key elements
5. Does not exist at all

Figure 5.2: Numbering scale model

3. *Graphical display model* – instead of using relative terms or numbers, graphical icons could be used to visually represent the scores. One example of this approach is the use of "Harvey Balls" which are round ideograms used for visual communication of qualitative information. *Figure 5.3* demonstrates the use of Harvey Balls for how well a project capability has been demonstrated during the assessment. In this example, the schedule management capability has some improvements recommended, whereas the scope management capability is found to be demonstrated and adequate.

Project Capability	Score	Themes
Schedule Management	◕	Plan missing dependencies and not updated
Scope Management	◕	Requirements complete and tracked
Resource Management	◑	Some gaps in team resources
Cost Management	◑	Tracking costs but not reporting on variances

○	◔	◑	◕	●
Capability not demonstrated	Capability improvements recommended	Capability improvements identified	Capability demonstrated and adequate	Capability demonstrated follows best practices

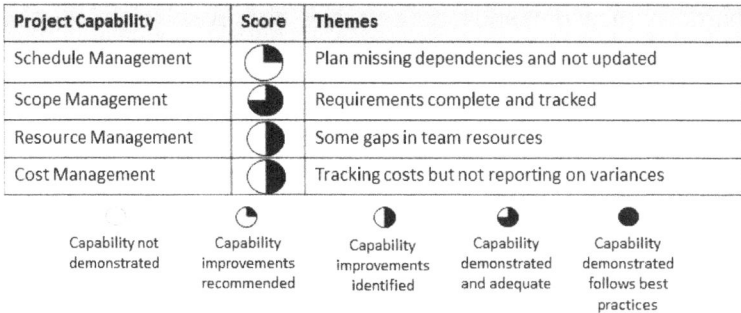

Figure 5.3: Harvey Ball model

Each of these types of assessment scoring models can be used to convey different information and messages. *Table 5.2* outlines some of those differences and considerations for using each of the scoring models.

Table 5.2: Assessment scoring model comparison

Scoring Model	Considerations
Relative Scoring	• Uses a small number of score categories so it is easy to see risk area differentiation • The tolerances for each score need to be well defined so that there is clarity in the differences between a low score and high score
Numbering Scale	• Uses several score values so may be better for distinguishing subtle differences in scores • Clear definition of scale is important
Graphical Display	• Good for demonstrating differences in scores and comparing them • More visually appealing so the presentation may appear more professional

Regardless of what type of scoring model is used for assessing information, this approach attempts to quantify, or show, the relative scores for each area of the project review. One challenge of this model is that sometimes it is hard to measure and score values for every risk, so the results may appear subjective and be questioned. The assessment team should ensure that there is a clear explanation for each score, and that there is a well defined set of criteria for determining each scored value.

Comparison to benchmark

A fourth approach for assessing information would be to compare the project findings to industry benchmarks for certain information. Robert C. Camp, in his book, *"Benchmarking: The Search for Industry Best Practices that Lead to Superior Performance"*, states that benchmarking can best be described as "the search for industry best practices that lead to superior performance" (Camp 1989). The assessment approach can include finding industry best practices for project management and delivery, and using those as a basis for comparing and scoring the project assessment against.

These best practices could include successful approaches used by other corporations, or metrics collected from industry research corporations that demonstrate top performing projects. There are several industry benchmarks which could be used to measure the project assessment findings, with some examples identified below:

• Process maturity models including models, such as Capability Maturity Model Integration (CMMI).

• Traditional project performance measures of schedule, cost and resources against project baselines.

• Quality measures, such as the Cost of Quality which measures the impact of delivering poor quality solutions.

- Advanced cost metrics, such as the Cost Performance Index which is a measure of project cost efficiency.

- Advanced schedule metrics, such as the Schedule Performance Index which is a measure of project schedule efficiency.

- Delivery quality metrics, such as defect identification rates and average defect resolution times.

Instead of the scoring for the assessment being based on assessor judgment or relative to subjective criteria, this scoring model allows for comparison to specific and recognized industry metrics. Therefore, this approach comes with a high level of credibility and the appearance of objectivity.

This subsection has identified four ways of approaching how to analyze the information collected from the project review. There are other approaches and these different aspects of these models can be leveraged and used together. The assessment team should consider the best way to approach the analysis based on scope, objectives and approach for the project review. Note that all of these assessment models should also allow for the recognition of where the project is performing well; the assessment should not just focus on deficiencies but rather be balanced in its findings.

5.2 What to look for

Once the assessment approach is determined, the team should review the findings to look for insights that can be used to populate the assessment framework. This can include specific themes in the findings, observations for how the project is being managed, or team member morale and perceptions.

Themes

There will be a lot of collected information to sort through and much of it will highlight common topics and appear to be repetitive, so the assessment team should look for these themes or trends. *Table 5.3* provides a set of examples of themes which could be identified on a project assessment.

Table 5.3: Types of themes that may be observed

Type	Description	Examples
Project Structure	Challenges with how the project is structured and teams are organized	• Unclear roles or responsibilities • Gaps in project accountabilities
Team Dynamics	Interpersonal or cultural challenges with team members	• Lack of stakeholder engagement • Interpersonal conflicts • Lack of trust
Process Deficiencies	Gaps or lack of clarity in delivery approach, documents or roles	• Documents not reviewed and signed off • Missed or incomplete deliverables
Lack of Diligence	Project management deliverables not being maintained properly	• Plans not being maintained • Open risks, issues and actions past due dates
Information Transparency	Areas where transparency of project information may not be sufficient	• Insufficient reporting of tracking to plan dates or finances • Lack of reporting on test cases of defects
Resource	There may be some	• Challenges with

Competency	resources who are struggling in their roles	performing activities • Inability to meet project commitments
Stakeholder Engagement	Challenges with sponsorship or leadership engagement	• Lack of decisions • Escalations of issues not being effective
Ineffective Communications	Not all stakeholders are receiving ample communications	• Confusion on the team • Conflicting understanding of status or risks

There are certainly many other possible themes and the assessment team should look to aggregate the findings into common results. Generally, when there are significant problems on a project, they reveal themselves in several different places but all tie back to the same root cause. The specific examples and symptoms that demonstrate the themes should be aligned to them, as this will become important when the team is packaging the report and will want to justify the findings.

How the project is being managed

Many project assessments investigate the "what" of the project including what documents are developed and what processes are followed. The assessment team should also consider looking at "how" the project is being managed. The project team could have the best defined PM and delivery processes but if they are not managing them properly, then the project can still have challenges. I wrote a book titled "*Applying Guiding Principles of Effective Program Delivery*" which focused on the key guiding principles of how to effectively manage a program (Wills 2013). Eight primary guiding principles were identified which are also areas that may need evaluating when conducting a project assessment.

1. Diligence

This guiding principle means that the project manager is staying on top of all of the moving parts of the project including keeping plans, risk logs, issue logs, action item logs, financials and decisions current, and ensuring that dates get met. Diligence can also include proactively managing activities, such as looking ahead at vendor contract expirations, resource start dates, future forecasts and upcoming purchases, to make sure that they are all tracking to the expected plan. Usually it is the project manager who has to think and track all of these items, so if we are not staying on top of all of them, then most likely they will not get the attention needed and possibly will not be completed on time or accurately.

This principle can be assessed by reviewing the key project deliverables to see how well they are maintained by the project team. Project plans which are not updated with progress or project RAID logs, with dates past the due date, could indicate a challenge with the diligence of the project team.

2. Attention to detail

Accompanying diligence is the principle of "paying attention to the details." If diligence is about providing structure and staying on top of all of the activities, then attention to detail is about understanding the specifics of those activities and making sure that the quality of the work is accurate and complete. This could include knowing the details of the scope and plan, or looking at the document specifics, such as confirming that all action items, issues, risks and plan activities have target dates and named owners associated with them, so that they can be assigned and tracked.

The assessment team should look for quality in the deliverables, such as financial information adding up, accurate content in status reports and maintaining detailed project plans. Consistent themes with not having proper details could indicate other problems on the project which need to be addressed.

3. Transparency
This principle is focused on gathering relevant project information and organizing it in a way that allows project stakeholders to understand themes, trends and risks to the project as early indicators of progress. This is important to have so that project managers have as much time as possible to take remediating action when a risk or issue arises. Transparency could include proper tracking and reporting of schedule progress, accomplishments, risks, issues and financial progress.

The assessment team should look to understand how project information is collected and how it is used to manage the project, with progress being reported out to stakeholders. Also, during the interviews they should pay attention to how well the stakeholders feel that they understand progress and risks, or can access that information to their satisfaction.

4. Single sources of truth
There is a lot of information on projects to manage and, therefore, the management of key project content becomes critical. As projects grow in size and as time passes, information gets spread in so many places that it becomes almost impossible to manage, let alone communicate to the

team. The guiding principle of having "single sources of truth" means storing all relevant project information in one location. This could mean having a single location for project scope, schedule, risks, issues, finances or resource information.

Each of the project management functions being reviewed should have authoritative sources of information and the assessment team should be looking for these in the documents. Team member interviews should also reveal clues as to what the sources of truth are for key project information and how well it is maintained.

5. Fact based decisions

This principle means being able to use facts and data to enable timely decisions and actions on a project. There are many decision points on a project related to scope, issue resolution, risk mitigation and solution recommendations. This guiding principle allows for decisions to be made effectively and in an informed way because there is a fact base to justify a particular option or recommendation.

The assessment should look at how decisions get made and issues or risks get mitigated, and what data is used to support the process. Some project documents may identity the supporting facts for decisions which may provide some insight. Other insights may have to be facilitated during the team member interviews.

6. The "ships" in the fleet of accountability

Accountability, as it relates to managing projects, can be grouped into three buckets that have words which all end in the letters "ship", so I refer to them as the ships in the "fleet of accountability" and the project manager is the captain of this fleet. They are *ownership* which means to truly take accountability for project outcomes, *stewardship* which is caring for the project and corporation, and *leadership* which is being a champion for the team and a leader on the project.

Each of these areas should be sought out in the project assessment. Because these are all characteristics of project leaders, they will have to be gathered through team member interviewing to look for relevant themes.

7. Simplicity
This principle is about keeping processes, technology solutions and organizations as simple as possible to avoid complexity, cost and confusion. On projects, complexity in any of these areas easily translates into more cost, more areas for issues to occur, and more risk to the ultimate delivery of the project. Consider the advice of Antoine de Saint-Exupery when he says that "It seems that perfection is achieved not when there is nothing more to add, but when there is nothing more to take away." He said this in the early 1900s and it is still an applicable approach today.

The assessment team should look to understand areas of complexity and highlight them as places which may require additional attention for risk, or even to seek to simplify. Some of these areas may be broader than the project, such as organizational or process complexity, but the review team should still identify them as areas to consider, even if they are broader enterprise recommendations.

8. Taking a customer focused approach
The final guiding principle is to take a customer focused approach to all project work and recognize where there are customer relationships with project stakeholders (e.g. the developer is a customer of the design documents and

requirements). The assessment team should try to understand what roles have a customer relationship and, through the interviews, determine how well they are working together.

Evaluating the "how" components can be challenging to discover as part of the assessment, since they are not as easy to find as looking to see if a particular document exists or not. However, they are important because they give insight into how well the project is being managed which has direct impact on the outcomes and success of the project. They also require the assessment team to be experienced in project management techniques so they can recognize if these principles are being applied.

Other considerations to look for

There may be other understandings that come out of the assessment of project information which would be relevant for the report. These additional areas should be recognized and contemplated as part of the assessment.

Intangibles

There can be intangibles on the project which are difficult to measure or quantify but which definitely have an impact on the project. The assessment team should be aware of these items when they are reviewing the project and seek to understand the impacts of them on the project, as they may be significant and worth highlighting.

- *Corporation cultures and norms* – corporations and organizations have distinctive cultures, practices and norms which may influence how team members behave and how the project work is managed. For example, in some corporation cultures showing yellow on a status report may be reflected as not being able to manage the project well which leads project managers to report on status as green when, in fact, it may not be.

- *Cultural conflicts* – cultures should also be considered when there is a project comprised of several different corporations who have different cultures which may be interacting with each other. For example, one corporation may have strong rigor around plans and process, whereas another may be more verbal and "loose" with process. In this case, the first corporation would be frustrated with the lack of planning for the second corporation, and the second corporation may feel overwhelmed with the process from the first.

- *Resource and team dynamics* – there may be undercurrents between team members that are possibly impacting project work. This could include fighting, different personalities and working styles, and a prior history of challenges between team members. Any of these items could impede the team's ability to work together, collaborate and communicate. The assessment should be sensitive to notice any team dynamics and point them out, especially if they are causing problems on the project.

- *Perception and reputations* – sometimes projects can have a reputation in the corporation beyond the project team. This can include a reputation of being a troubled project, working team members too hard, or not meeting commitments. The assessment may want to consider seeking to understand if the project being reviewed has a reputation around the corporation and then look to determine the causes of these perceptions.

- *Morale* – projects are critically dependent on the team members to be successful. Therefore, projects which have a low morale on the team should be considered to have significant risk, as team members may leave, feel overwhelmed and produce poor quality work, or just give up altogether. The project assessment should consider the morale and energy of the team as an indicator of success or problems.

Conflicting information

The document reviews and interviews will yield a significant amount of information regarding the project. At times, some of this information may appear to be in conflict with other information gathered. The assessment team should identify where this happens and investigate further to understand the conflicts and determine what the correct information is. In some cases, this conflict may be a notable item to call out in the report if it demonstrates a key point, such as confusion of information or lack of transparency. Some examples of conflicting information are noted below:

- Team member interviews identifying information which is conflicting with another team member.

- Team members saying one thing but documents saying another. The team could think there are no challenges in a particular area, and yet the risk log or issues log may demonstrate otherwise.

- Stakeholders getting one update and believing one set of information but project documents and team members having a different view.

- Several documents having conflicting information, such as different dates for the same milestone.

- Status report for milestones may indicate that an activity is complete but the project plan is not marked as 100% for that activity.

- Status may show that a project is in green status but other project deliverables (e.g. risk log, issues log, financial reporting and project plan milestone progress) may indicate additional challenge areas which would suggest that the project is not in green status.

Looking for these conflicts is useful for the assessment because it demonstrates some of the challenges which the team may be having, but then uses the facts and documents to support the findings and determine the true story.

Enterprise recommendations

Since the assessment will be reviewing many aspects of the project, it may reveal existing challenges with how the corporation operates, beyond the specifics of the individual project. These more broad observations should be captured separately, with some recommended areas to consider for the corporation. Some examples could include the following types of recommendations:

- *Interdivision operating model* – projects are usually comprised of personnel from several different organizations who have to work together. The project assessment may reveal some challenges in the operating model between these divisions and could highlight these, with some recommendations to improve those interactions.

- *Process improvements* – most corporations have a software delivery lifecycle with a standard set of processes and deliverables. The assessment may reveal opportunities to improve some of these processes in the standard framework.

- *Stewardship opportunities* – the project being reviewed may have developed new management tools or deliverables which would be good to share with other projects, and should be recommended for the corporation standard framework. The project may also have very good examples of standard deliverables which should be submitted for framework as well.

Since the objective of the assessment is most likely focused on the project and not the broader corporation, the assessment team should determine the best way to present any enterprise findings or recommendations. It may make sense to have a separate set of findings that get documented and presented to a different team of stakeholders, instead of grouping these findings with the project specific ones. This could be collected as part of a corporation wide initiative to capture project lessons learned, and the spirit of continuous improvement of the corporation standard delivery methodology.

5.3 Determine recommendations

After the collected information has been analyzed and assessed for themes, gaps, key findings and insights, the team should identify a set of recommendations. This is where the experience of the assessment team members and the industry best practices should be used to propose actions that the project can take to remediate risks and resolve issues. There are many different categories of recommendations and next steps that the assessment team could identify; some of which are documented below:

- *Additional structure* – the assessment may find that the

program structure, roles or responsibilities require additional clarification, or changes, to become more effective. For example, a certain troubled area of the project may require additional oversight, or resources, to help manage that work.

- *Resource changes* – the project may have resources who are not the right "fit" for the role that they are in, and it is having an impact on the project. In these cases, resources may have to be changed. This may also include changing the allocations to resources, where some critical resources may need to focus more on the project and have an increased allocation to the project.

- *Planning or replanning* – the assessment may find that the current plans are not realistic and may suggest revisiting the plans, validating the scope, and possibly recasting the schedule and milestones. This may also include reviewing the scope and looking for opportunities to remove or defer scope, as a means of helping a troubled project get back on schedule or budget.

- *Improved communications* – in cases where information was not clear to the project team, there may be recommendations about better team member engagement and an updated communication plan.

- *End to end reviews* – there may be some requirements or solutions which are at risk, or are very complex which could require a thorough end to end review of scenarios, design and testing solutions, to ensure that any gaps, or risks, get identified and acted upon.

- *Focus on quality* – in cases where there are findings regarding the quality of deliverables or outputs, the assessment could recommend additional actions to improve quality, such as document reviews or formal gates and sign offs.

- *Ensure standards and consistency* – if the project review was looking at adherence to corporation standards, there may be some recommendations around improving the alignment of the deliverables to the standards and better consistency.

- *Productivity tools* – the team may have some additional tools or processes that they would recommend to improve its productivity. For example, more robust financial or schedule tracking.

- *Actions to close* – there will probably also be several outstanding actions which require attention, such as missed plan dates and outstanding issues, risks, or actions that need to be closed.

- *Simplification* – complexity drives risk, so if the assessment finds that the processes or technology solutions are too complex, they may want to propose some recommendations around simplifying those items. This will allow the team to focus better on the important areas, and will also remove some of the challenges associated with complex solutions or processes.

- *Make decisions* – the review may highlight some outstanding decisions which need to be made, and there could be recommendations to do so, which would allow the project to progress past a stated challenge.

- *Further analysis* – even with the document reviews and team member interviews, there may still be follow ups for further understanding and assessment. The assessment team should identify when there are additional review areas or analysis suggested, and the reasoning for them. For example, the team may suggest a technology deep dive review into a solution that appears to be risky.

These identified categories represent just a few samples of possible recommended actions which could arise from the project review. The assessment team will need to carefully think through what actions they would recommend against each of the project findings. To that end, there are some considerations that the assessment team should contemplate when determining which recommendations they will be proposing to the project.

Prioritize the recommendations

There will most likely be many recommendations in the assessment and they will not all have equal impact on the project, so it may make sense to identify the impact and somehow prioritize or weight the recommendations accordingly. The suggested actions should be aligned to specific findings, with a priority assigned to them in terms of criticality of impact, or immediacy of need. This identification will allow the team to focus on those actions which have the most immediate and highest possible impact on project success. For example, a risk in meeting project commitments should have higher priority actions than recommendations to align document formats to corporation standards.

Identify a sense of effort

The recommended actions should also come with some measure of effort to implement which could be identified in effort hours, duration, additional resources and possibly even cost. This would give the stakeholders a sense of what it would take to implement the suggestion, and they could then decide whether or not to pursue them. Not all recommendations can be easily estimated, so the assessment team should determine when it is appropriate to provide effort and when they should not include this information. Instead of specific estimates, the team may also want to consider having a "high", "medium" and "low" value of effort assigned to each of the actions.

Demonstrate and justify the value

The recommendations should be treated as a set of proposals which the assessment team is trying to convince the stakeholders to approve. Therefore, the recommendations should clearly state the value and show how they solve problems, and why the project team should perform them. For example, suggested focus on diligence with managing a project plan should call out that proper tracking of the plan provides early indicators of problems which allows time for management to take action and avoid further delays. This statement would be much more appealing to stakeholders than just "track your plan."

Beyond stating the description and value of the recommendation, the team should also look to somehow justify them. This could include referencing industry standard best practices or material. This can bring credibility to the recommended action and substantiate the suggested value.

Keep them practical

Project assessment recommendations should be practical which includes considering the phase of the project, the culture of the organization, and the impact or value. For example, suggesting for a project to update requirement templates when it is in the testing phase and nearly complete, would not be a sound recommendation, even if the finding was valid that the standard formats were not used. Also, given that the time when projects are assessed is usually when the project is under way, the team is probably busy, so the recommendations should be considerate of their time.

Determine how they will be tracked

The project review should not end with handing off a set of recommendations and a hearty handshake. To close the loop on the assessment, there should be a method and plan for tracking progress against the recommended actions, to ensure that they get implemented. This approach should be agreed to as part of the process, as well as confirmed with the final report and presentation.

In conclusion, each finding and theme documented in the project assessment should have a recommendation, or proposed action, to take against it. Once the team has identified the recommendations and aligned them to the discoveries, they are ready to package them into the report.

CHAPTER 6: PACKAGE AND PRESENT

The final step in the project assessment process is to package the findings and recommendations and then present them to project stakeholders. This is where everything comes together and tells the story about the project including risks and opportunities, so this step is significant as there are many ways to organize the materials.

6.1 Approach

The assessment report should be organized in such a way that it is easy to read, has a logical flow, and conveys the key messages of the review. There are several sections which are typically used in a project assessment report. These are highlighted in *Table 6.1*, along with the intent and common content contained in each section.

Table 6.1: Typical sections of the assessment report

Section	Intent	Content
Context	Describes the objectives and background of the assessment and the project	• Background of assessment • Objectives
Approach	Outlines the approach taken for the assessment	• Steps in the approach • Documents reviewed • People interviewed
Executive Summary	High level findings, themes and recommendations	• Summary of findings • Summary of recommendations
Detailed Findings	Describes each key finding and theme with examples	• Findings organized by category • Scoring model, if

		appropriate
Detailed Recommendations	Describes the recommended action for each finding	• Specific actions to take with impact, value and priority • A plan for implementing the suggested actions
Supporting Documents	Any additional materials needed to support the findings or recommendations (usually in appendix)	• Supporting documents • Additional evidence and examples

Each of the project assessment report sections should have a clear purpose of what content and messages should be conveyed. They should be organized and structured to present the assessment information, keeping in mind the stakeholders and audience that the report will be provided to.

Context

The assessment report should start with a section on the context of the project review. This can include the stated objectives of the assessment, some background and history on the project being reviewed, or the current state of the project. This is important as it will "ground" the audience of the report, and remind them of the purpose and intent for which the report was being conducted. This will also serve as an introduction for those reviewing the assessment report without a formal presentation.

If there were specific goals and objectives given from stakeholders for the assessment, then this section would reiterate them as the starting point for the remainder of the findings. This also allows other stakeholders to understand the goals before going into details, so their expectations can be set as to what will be in the report.

Approach

The assessment report should also contain a section on the approach taken for the project review. This will give stakeholders a sense of how the assessment was conducted, with the key activities, as well as what information was reviewed. *Figure 6.1* shows an example of a visual representation for the assessment approach with each of the steps, and a corresponding description and listing of inputs and outputs. Note that many corporations may have a standard framework for assessments but this will still be a good way to remind the audience of the review process and associated steps.

	1. Review Project Documents	2. Conduct Team Interviews	3. Analyze Findings	4. Determine Recommendations	5. Document Results and Report Out
Description	Review project documents to understand the approach and review the quality of the deliverables	Interview a cross-section of the team to gage the project approach and perceptions	Review the information to look for trends, best practices, and areas of improvement	Determine recommendations for improvement of opportunities and mitigation of risks	Package the analysis and recommendations and present to key stakeholders
Inputs	▪ Project documents ▪ Company framework	▪ Interviews with key team members ▪ Question inventory	▪ Deliverable review ▪ Interview notes	▪ Inventory of key observations and trends ▪ PM best practices	▪ Analysis information ▪ Recommendations
Deliverables / Outputs	▪ Assessment of project deliverables	▪ Interview notes	▪ Inventory of key observations and trends	▪ Recommendations	▪ Final presentation

Figure 6.1: Chart of assessment approach steps

This section can also include content listing all documents which were reviews, and the names and roles of the team members who were interviewed. This will provide credibility to the assessment, and highlight where the assessment findings were derived from for the stakeholders of the review.

Note that the approach section can be put in several areas of the final project assessment report. It could go in the front of the assessment report to explain the approach taken, before getting into specifics, or it could be put in the appendix as a reference. The order will depend on how the assessment team wants to tell the story, and the audience of the report who may be familiar with the approach.

Executive summary

Project assessments can have a lot of information, discoveries, recommendations and next steps which can make the final report very detailed and large in size. There should be a section which provides an "executive summary" of the key findings and recommendations. The executive summary should be at a high level and succinct so that a senior stakeholder can read it and understand the important messages from the review, without having to look at all of the details. Some examples of the type of content which should be in the executive summary could include the following:

- The most impactful findings and themes, such as significant schedule risks, cost overruns, resource challenges or scope misses.
- Noteworthy metrics that demonstrate risk, such as comparison of project results to industry metrics.
- Call out any substantial positive themes with the project, such as the ability to meet commitments given challenges and complexities.

- The key proposed recommendations and next steps for the project team to implement the actions.

This section should be developed after the detailed sections are developed, since the content will need to be "rolled up" from those sections. The assessment team should consider the audience and recognize what messages they want to articulate, before documenting the executive summary.

Detailed findings

The core of the assessment report will be the detailed findings section. This section should organize, and contain, the project information that was collected from document reviews and team member interviews.

The detailed findings section could start with a summary that shows the categories of the assessment with the score and high level points, as demonstrated in *Figure 6.2*. In this example, there are six categories that were being reviewed and scored. One was deemed adequate (full shading), one had improvements needed (empty shading), and the rest had notable opportunities or risks (partial shading).

Category	Rating	Themes
Scope Management	◔	• Scope not documented in one place • Many scope changes after signoff
Schedule Management	●	• Schedule is documented and maintained • Some activities not complete and past due
Resource Management	◔	• Some gaps in the resource plan • Not all roles and responsibilities understood
Cost Management	○	• Financial reporting not comprehensive • Project is over budget by 20%
Communication Management	◔	• Communication plan exists • Not all stakeholders feel informed on status
RAID Management	◔	• Risks, issues and actions tracked • Many items open for several weeks

● Adequate   ◔ Opportunities/Risks   ○ Needs Improvement

Figure 6.2: Summary of findings

The summary of findings is a good way to show an aggregation of the findings across the assessment categories. Then, there could be one page for each of the detailed findings within the assessment categories. An example of this construct is demonstrated in *Figure 6.3* which is a drill down into the Scope Management section. In this case, this area was scored as having opportunities or risks. The top section of the chart shows the focus of this section, which includes scope documents, change control documents, and interviews with key team members. The second section calls out the key themes that were discovered during the assessment, as well as the key points which substantiate that theme. In this case, there is a mix of document findings and quotes from interviews.

Category: Scope Management	Score: ⊕ Opportunities/Risks

Focus Areas	• Scope Planning • Scope Definition • Scope Control • Change Management Documents • Interview Business Analysts, Subject Matter Experts and Project Managers

Themes	Examples/ Evidence
Scope is not well documented or in one place	• Four different documents, in different locations, house requirements • No clear traceability between scope documents and others • "What I have read for scope and what I have heard are different" – Project Manager • "I have no idea what the scope is definitively; high level I know, but not the details. It is not located in one place" – Business Analyst
Scope is changing often and after signoffs	• "Stakeholders change their mind a lot...they change their mind about what is important on the fly" – Business Analyst • Change Management log shows 20 new changes to scope after the requirements were signed off • Requirements documents are not updated after changes get approved

Figure 6.3: Detailed findings

The detailed findings are important to the assessment because they provide the insight into the findings which then drive the assessment report and project recommendations. There are a few concepts that should be contemplated when packaging the detailed findings for the project assessment:

- *Support themes with examples* – examples are critical to highlight and justify the themes and scoring in the project assessment. It is a possibility that someone from the project team will argue with the scoring, or the theme, as they may not understand the details of the challenges, or may not want the report to somehow look negatively on them to their management. Having examples and quotes from team members will help make the review more credible and minimize the debate over the validity.

- *Quantify where possible* – having examples for themes of findings is important but the assessment team should also look to quantify them as much as possible, and make them based on specific facts.

- *Use benchmarks* – examples should also be compared to industry benchmarks where possible. These are good measures that can be used to demonstrate themes, or justify points in the assessment.

- *Additional pages* – in some cases, a theme or key finding will require a specific call out and page which does not follow the same structure as the other pages in the detailed findings section. These could be very helpful as additional evidence, or visual, to demonstrate to stakeholders. For example, the assessment team may want to add a page that has a financial report, to demonstrate variances or significant financial challenges. Another example could be a diagram which shows gaps, or overlaps, in responsibilities in the context of the project team structure.

The detailed findings section should be the largest section of the assessment report, and should be structured to call out the themes, specific details, associated scoring and evidence. One approach could be to organize it as a summary, and then go into each section, as *Figures 6.3* and *6.4* highlight. Other approaches may include documenting the findings in text, with supporting bullets, or attaching project documents as evidence. However the content is represented, this section should be well organized and easy to follow, since it provides the content and examples for the entire report.

Detailed recommendations

Once the findings are organized and documented, the next section of the report should identify the recommendations against those findings. *Figure 6.4* follows the example in

Figure 6.3 and shows the recommendations for the themes identified in the Scope Management category of the project assessment. Each of the themes has a set of recommendations identified by the assessment team as possible actions to take to improve the project in the respective review theme.

Category: Scope Management		Score: ⊕ Opportunities/Risks

Focus Areas	<ul><li>Scope Planning</li><li>Scope Definition</li><li>Scope Control</li><li>Change Management Documents</li><li>Interview Business Analysts, Subject Matter Experts and Project Managers</li></ul>

Themes	Recommendations
Scope is not well documented or in one place	<ul><li>Create a centralized scope document and have the stakeholders agree to it</li><li>Revalidate that we have the correct scope with the correct customers (may need to prioritize) and then have them commit to it</li></ul>
Scope is changing often and after signoffs	<ul><li>Document scope and change approach with project management approach</li><li>Enforce signatures and impact analysis of changes and document on the change log</li></ul>

Figure 6.4: Detailed recommendations

This example only states what the recommendations are, without any qualifications. The assessment team may also want to provide more information around the impact, value, or priority of the recommendations as well, especially if there are a lot of recommendations, and the team wants to call out specific ones to focus on. This should be contemplated based on the number of recommendations, the assessment team's judgment, the audience of the report, and the objectives of the project assessment.

The assessment team may also want to have a section that lists out a specific action plan against the recommendations. *Figure 6.5* is an example of what this action plan could look like and shows several actions, organized by category, with the identified action owner and timing to complete. This can be useful as a takeaway from the assessment for a specific plan and set of next steps which can then be tracked and reported on back to project management and stakeholders.

Category	Action	Owner	Timing
Program Structure	Update the roles and responsibilities matrix with key roles and names	M. Jones	Feb 15
Scope Management	Create a centralized scope document and have the stakeholders agree to it	J. Smith	March 1
Scope Management	Document scope and change approach with project management approach	J. Smith	March 1
Finance Management	Development of tracking tool for reporting financial variances	M. Jordan	April 1

Figure 6.5: Action plan

The detailed recommendations section is the part of the assessment where specific actions are identified, and so they should be clear, align to the themes, and provide specific next steps for the project team to follow.

Supporting documents

In addition to the context, approach, findings and recommendations, the assessment team may want to include some additional documents in the report. This could include documents which demonstrate some of the more impactful findings of the review, such as specific metrics around financial variances, documentation of significant scope changes, or framework processes which were not followed properly.

Other documents could support recommended next steps, such as a proposed updated team structure diagram, or a suggested plan for next steps around restructuring a project or program. *Figure 6.6* shows an example of a high level plan for reorganizing a program and reconfirming scope that was used in the case study from section 4.1.5. This plan identifies the major steps required, with the supporting key activities underneath them, and the overall duration for each of these activities.

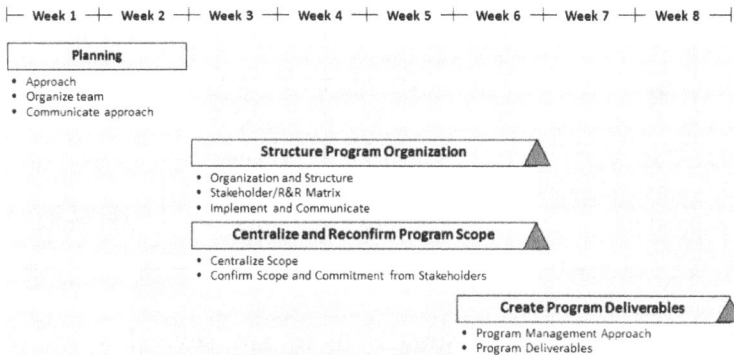

Figure 6.6: Example of a planning schedule

Other supporting documents could include project document examples, such as the most recent status report, prior audit histories, or current financial snapshot. The assessment team should identify documents which they think are relevant for the report, or required as part of the objectives, and add them to the supporting materials.

6.2 Packaging the content

The assessment report should tell a story, and be organized based on the goals, approach used and target audience. While most assessment reports contain the sections outlined in Section 6.1, the order of those sections may differ. This could be a result of many factors including corporation culture, stakeholder preference or organization standards. *Table 6.2* shows some ways to organize the content based on three possible approaches, and identifies the numeric sequencing of the sections.

Table 6.2: Possible organization of sections

Section	Executive Report	Build Up	Punch Line First
Context	1	1	1
Approach	Appendix	2	Appendix
Executive Summary	2	6	2
Detailed Findings	Appendix	3	3
Detailed Recommendations	Appendix	4	4
Supporting Documents	Appendix	5	Appendix

As *Table 6.2* demonstrates, there are several ways to organize the materials based on the approach for packaging and presenting them, as well as considerations for the stakeholders being presented to. The assessment team needs to consider how they want to organize the materials to most effectively align to their audience and stakeholder's expectations and preferences.

Executive report

When presenting the findings to senior executives, it may be best to keep the report at a high level and focus on major themes, findings and recommendations. The report should still set the context first, to ground the stakeholders in the objectives and intent of the assessment. Then the executive summary should be the focal point of the conversation. The remainder of the materials should be kept in supplemental documents or the appendix, for reference, should the conversation warrant a discussion on those topics.

This approach allows for a succinct and focused meeting that calls out the most impactful points, which is generally what executives are looking for. There should also be a clear set of next steps and a discussion around how to report back progress against these recommendations and associated actions.

Build up

Another style of packaging the assessment material could be an approach where the story is "built up" in a sequential manner. In this approach the report would start with the context, then explain the approach used, then identify the detailed findings, followed by the detailed recommendations and supporting documents. Lastly, the summary would be used to recap the key points from the prior sections.

This approach is good for detail oriented stakeholders who may want more of a sequential story of how the assessment was conducted, what was found, and what the recommendations are. This may also be good for stakeholders who are not familiar with the project, and would want to understand the story of the assessment and the project.

Punch line first and then details

A third approach would be to start with the summary (or "punch line") first and then identify the details which support the summary. In this case, the focus of the presentation would be on the summary of findings, after first stating the context. Then it would get into the details and evidence which supports that summary.

This approach may work well for stakeholders familiar with the project who want to "cut to the chase" on the findings and recommendations and not dwell in the details. The details would still be provided as justification for summary points.

Considerations

There are several aspects that the assessment team should contemplate when packaging the content, to ensure that the report conveys the appropriate messages to the stakeholders when being presented.

- *Corporation culture* – some corporations have cultural characteristics which would influence how the assessment report was packaged, presented and received. For example, they may be sensitive to reporting problems, or be perceived as placing blame, so the report may want to be packaged in a way that highlights positives and sensitively demonstrates risks and challenges.

- *Stakeholder's personal style* – if there is a primary stakeholder who the report will be presented to, it may be a good idea to understand their style of communication. For example, seeing if they like detailed information, if they look for the summary first, or they like metrics and numbers. Understanding their style will yield better results, since it will be more aligned with how they want to receive and process information.

- *Several versions of the report* – given that projects can have many stakeholders, there may have to be several different versions of the assessment report for different audiences. For example, an executive summary would be used for senior leaders but the more detailed findings would be used for the project management and team members who want to see the specifics of the report.

- *Corporation standards* – corporations may have existing standard templates, or formats, for project assessments which may prescribe the structure needed to package the project assessment report.

- *Tie back to objectives* – the assessment team should make sure that the final report addresses all of the stated objectives of the review, and that the report clearly demonstrates this.

- *Get early feedback* – it may be a good idea to pass along some of the draft findings to the project manager or leads, to get their view and acceptance on the findings. These initial reactions may help to better package the findings, or drill deeper into some areas. They would also minimize some of the shock factor later, and the situation where the entire report gets questioned at the final presentation.

6.3 Presenting

Once the project assessment report has been developed and packaged, the review team may have to present the findings to multiple, different, project stakeholders. This could include a formal presentation, distribution of the report, or a meeting to walk through the findings. There are several considerations when presenting the final assessment report, with several of them highlighted below.

Stakeholders and cadence of presentations

Often, there are many stakeholders who have an interest in the project review. The assessment team should be sure to understand who they are, and contemplate them when determining the communication plan for the report. *Table 6.3* identifies several project stakeholders and some examples of areas which they may possibly have an interest in regarding the assessment report and findings.

Table 6.3: Project review stakeholders

Stakeholder	Possible Interest
Project Manager	• Understand possible risks in delivering project and identification of actions to close them • Understand key messages from review as a reflection on their success in managing the project
Project IT Lead, Business Lead and Sponsor	• Understand key risk areas and gaps that pose risks to the project meeting commitments • Identify progress of project functions compared against industry benchmarks • Gain insights into actions or decisions that they could take to improve the success of the project
Project Team Members	• Understand if their concerns are being heard • Understand what actions will be taken by management
Corporation Standards Organizations	• Understand adherence to the delivery framework and standards • Look for possible best practices and examples to supplement existing framework
Corporation Internal Audit	• Look for any corporation exposure points or risks (e.g. controls or financial reporting)

Based on the stakeholder assessment, the review team should determine a communication plan that contains the appropriate cadence for presenting the report to these stakeholders. This may include feeding some of the key findings to project leadership, as the assessment is being conducted as part of the regular report outs. This would minimize some of the "shock factor" of having all of the content presented at the end of the assessment, however, there is risk that the content may not be fully vetted before communicating it early.

Also, the project team, or project manager, should be able to review the assessment report first, to identify any initial concerns or reactions. Note that the presentation and review process should allow for project team members to document any discrepancies, or facts, which they think are incorrect, or require additional clarification. Then, the report should be presented to the senior leads on the program, and finally the executives or sponsors. The report should also be made available to the project team members, unless there is sensitive information which requires discretion.

Approach for presenting

Once the cadence of stakeholder presentations has been determined, the assessment team should plan out how to articulate the information to the stakeholders. There are several ways that the team can review the report with stakeholders:

- *Distribute and then discuss* – the assessment team can distribute the final project report beforehand, to allow stakeholders to review it and then set up a meeting to discuss specific questions and concerns. This model may work well with the project team, so they get a chance to review the findings in detail and come prepared to discuss them with the review team.

- *Detailed report with high level presentation* – in this approach, the assessment team develops a high level presentation to call out the key findings, themes, recommendations and next steps, and then uses the more detailed assessment report as a reference. This approach may work well for high level management who want to understand the key points, but not have to go through a very detailed report.
- *Walk through the detailed report* – this approach entails having the assessment team walk through the detailed project report and review each section. This may work with the project management team that would want to really understand the findings and ensure that the proper actions are taken to close the gaps.

The assessment team should determine the best approach to present the information with the project team and sponsor of the assessment. This should be understood early on in the assessment, as it will influence how the final project assessment report gets packaged and presented.

Also considering the approach, the assessment team should plan for specific responsibilities during the presentation so that the conversation runs smoothly and as planned. There are several roles to consider for the presentation:

- *Facilitator* – there should be one person facilitating the conversation to ensure that the agenda gets followed, key discussion points and takeaways get documented, and that the conversation progresses. This person should be a good communicator and be able to read the audience to see how well they are following along, and moderate the pace of the conversation accordingly.
- *Presenters* – determine who is presenting what content

and for how long, so that expectations are clear before the presentation occurs. Based on the presentation content and who conducted the assessment, there may be different presenters for different sections of the report.

- *Experts* – the assessment team may want to have some experts attend the report out so they can provide insight in specific functional areas, or domains, if the conversation warrants it. For example, if there are technology specific findings, then the team may want a technology expert or architect there to discuss best practices and recommendations based on their experiences. This also demonstrates a level of experience and credibility with the team and therefore the report.

- *Note taker* – there will most likely be takeaways, actions and clarifications required so there should be someone at the presentation who is capturing the notes and next steps from the conversation. This is important and should be a separate role so that the team members can focus on the conversation and not on trying to capture all of the points at the same time as presenting.

Determining the approach for the presentation is important and allows the assessment team to plan for how the report will be presented, and what roles team members will play during the presentation. This should allow for an effective presentation that meets the stakeholders' expectations and comes across as professional and credible.

Consider the audience

The assessment team should be very conscious of the audience when presenting the report. This includes understanding any politics, cultural, or interpersonal sensitivities. For example, a project manager may feel that the assessment is a criticism of their ability to manage the project, and may feel "attacked" if the report is reviewed with them and their management, or customers, in the same room. In this case, the presenter should recognize this and articulate the findings in a way to not seem like personal attacks which could include the use of facts, or examples, to highlight the points.

The facilitator and presenters should also be aware of how the audience is responding to the presentation and maybe even modify their approach, as appropriate. For example, some audience members may start looking ahead at the materials, or not seem focused on specific details, and the facilitator may want to speed up the pace of the conversation, defer non-relevant conversations, or try a different approach to engage them.

Be prepared

When communicating the report, the presenter will want to be deeply familiar with the content. This will allow them to present effectively and react properly as the conversation evolves. This may require the use of facts and examples to justify a point that someone is questioning and seeking to understand better. It also may require referencing an industry benchmark, or report, to highlight a point.

The worst thing that a presenter could do would be to look unprepared or disorganized. This makes the entire presentation and report start to lose credibility, regardless of how good the project assessment was.

Have clear next steps

Lastly, the presentation should end with an agreement on specific next steps and actions. This should be part of the discussion and be documented so that there are clear expectations. These next steps may include the following possible activities:

- *Follow ups from the conversation* – based on the level of detail during the conversation, there will probably be clarifications required, additional follow ups, and other action items that get discussed. These items should be captured with specific timings and owners for each one.

- *Additional assessments* – during the discussion, the project stakeholders may ask for additional reviews of specific areas which would start the assessment process over again. These would probably be more detailed and specialized. For example, a review of a specific architecture solution component or product.

- *Future checkpoints* – given that there will be recommendations and takeaways from the conversation, the teams should agree on next steps around obtaining status on these items. This may require a status report being sent out, or a series of meetings that get scheduled to discuss the actions.

This chapter was dedicated to the packaging and presenting of the assessment report. There are many approaches and considerations for the team to contemplate, and it is not as simple as dumping all of the content into a document and passing it out. The approach for packaging the report, and presenting the report, needs to be carefully considered and planned for so that the final report has credibility, and the assessment is viewed as being valuable and insightful.

CHAPTER 7: SUMMARY

Delivering on projects is becoming critical to the success of corporations today, given the large investments and bets that corporations are making with technology. At the same time, the complexity and size of the technology, and therefore the projects, is growing. Project assessments are an important tool for corporations to use to take checkpoints on projects, measure the success of them, and identify key risks in a timely manner so as to be able to take course correcting action.

This book has focused on the approach for assessing a project, as well as supplemented each of the chapters with multiple considerations, or important concepts, for the assessment team to contemplate. There is no "one size fits all" model to assessments and so the reader will need to take into consideration the key points and references from this book, and use it with their own judgment and experience to conduct their assessments. This final chapter will recap the key messages from the book, aggregate some of the key concepts into checklists for easy reference, and provide some additional references for further insight.

7.1 Key points

There are several pervasive topics that get repeated throughout the book which are important concepts to reflect on when preparing for, or conducting, a project assessment. They will be summarized in this section as a reminder.

Tie back to objectives

The project assessment should have a defined set of objectives and goals, and all of the materials produced should tie back to these objectives. During every step of the process the assessment team should remember these objectives and ensure that they are working in a manner to directly meet them.

- The plan and approach for the review should be organized in a way to ensure that the objectives get met.

- The collecting of information should align to gathering insights into areas of focus for the objectives.

- The recommendations should also be focused on providing actions against the areas of focus for the objectives.

- Lastly, the presentation should be packaged and presented in a way as to directly address the objectives.

The review team should ensure that the project assessment objectives get established early on and are clear, so that the team can work towards them for the remainder of the assignment and align all work to meeting them.

Be prepared

During every step of the assessment process, the team should ensure that they perform significant preparation and planning.

- *The plan* – preparing the assessment approach and plan will allow the team to focus on the most important aspects of the project being reviewed, and be organized during the entire assessment process. This will also optimize the time of the team members, so they spend time on the most impactful activities.

- *Interviews* – proper planning will allow the assessment team to understand who the key team members will be to interview, have well thought out questions, and focus the conversation on the more critical aspects of the project review.

- *Document collection* – spending time upfront on planning the document reviews will enable the team to go after the most relevant and important documents, and look for the most impactful insights from them.

- *Assess and recommend* – having a well thought out plan will assist the team to focus on the most important information to assess, which will also result in high quality and impactful recommendations.

- *Presentation* – spending time on preparing for the presentation will result in a presentation that is tailored to the right audience, conveys the important messages, and will be received well by the audience.

Being prepared during all of these activities will produce a better project assessment and ultimately result in better outcomes for the project. The preparation and planning should be viewed as an investment which will yield good rewards. Plus, it demonstrates the level of rigor and planning which the assessment is looking for in the projects, and therefore does not appear hypocritical that the assessment team lacks the structure that they are reviewing and recommending.

Look for themes

The assessment will reveal many findings and collect a significant amount of information. The assessment team should look to group this information into themes that are pervasive, recurring, or repeat themselves often. The themes should be supported with evidence and examples from the collection of information. Grouping these items into themes enables the assessment to demonstrate that these findings are not just identified in one place, but occur in several places and therefore warrant proper attention. Finally, the team should identify recommendations that address the overall theme, as well as individual actions for specific findings which require attention.

The packaging of the presentation and materials should anchor on these themes, and use them to identify the key points of the assessment, demonstrate them with specific examples, and then align specific recommendations and next steps to them.

Look for the "how"

The project assessment should go beyond just confirming if specific documents exist, or that certain process steps are followed. The assessment should get into how the project is being managed, and how the documents and standards are being used to ensure proper management of the work and transparency of challenges.

Paying attention to how the project is being managed will require the team to ask specific questions during the interviews, and review documents, looking for certain insights. It has to be a deliberate strategy which is encompassed in the assessment approach, but with this method the findings will be much more impactful, and relevant, to enable the project to meet its objectives successfully. Projects don't fail because they use the wrong standard format or don't follow processes to the letter; they fail because they have problems managing the complexities and specifics properly.

Once the "how" items are identified, the team can then recommend practical actions to improve these challenges. This may include structural changes in the project, role modifications, additional processes or tools, or improvements in the project operational methods and documents.

Use facts and examples

The project assessment will reveal many interesting findings and observations. These key points should be substantiated through facts and examples. There are several different types of evidence which could be used to do this.

- Specific details from project documents, such as financial information, scope elements and project schedule content.

- Examples of documents which demonstrate particular themes, such as plans and issues logs which are not maintained properly.

- Industry benchmarks which can be used to compare to characteristics of the project being assessed.

- Facts related to recommended actions, such as industry metrics for the ratios of time spent in particular project phases in the example, where the recommendation would be to modify where the team is spending its time.

Focusing on the facts yields multiple benefits for the assessment and the team conducting the project review.

- *Demonstrate the themes* – since themes are comprised of aggregations of specific points, having examples validates, and supports, the key messages identified by the theme found in the assessment.

- *Justifies points* – because the assessment will reveal gaps and challenges, some team members may be sensitive and argue with the findings and, therefore, having specific examples can provide the justification.

- *Demonstrates value* – several recommendations will be identified during the assessment process, and facts, or industry benchmarks, can be used to influence the stakeholders as to the value and impact of these actions.

- *Adds credibility* – facts and examples provide substantiation to the assessment so that the findings are not viewed as subjective but rather based on specific facts, documents, and supporting evidence. This adds credibility to the assessment and the key messages in the report.

In summary, it is good practice to leverage facts and evidence for assessing the project information, proposing recommended actions, and then packaging and presenting the final assessment report.

Tailor the assessment

Another concept that has been pervasive in this book has been the theme of "tailoring" the assessment. While project assessments can have a formal structure and standard checklist or plan, they should be flexible to modify the approach based on the nuances of the corporation, project, stakeholders, and audience. These should be considered during each step of the assessment process.

- *Approach* – the approach should consider the stakeholders, and goals, and craft the plan to meet their needs. For example, the stakeholders may be more interested in controlling cost than in project management best practices, and so the assessment should spend more time on assessing financial health and risks.

- *Interviews* – the interviews should also be tailored to the specific goals of the objectives and confirmed assessment approach. Also, based on previous reviews of project materials, the assessment team may want to modify the interview questions to focus on specific clarifications or early observations.

- *Documents* – similar to the interviews, the document reviews should be customized based on the scope and approach for the assessment, to look for insights related to the objectives. Not all documents will have equal value to the assessment so the team should modify their approach to look for the most impactful information.

- *Packaging* – the assessment report should be packaged with the objectives and audience in mind. The stakeholders may have specific preferences for how the report should be organized or flow which the team will need to consider and plan for.

- *Presentation* – the presenting of the final report will also need to be adapted to the styles of the audience which may include the use of visual aids, presentation of examples, or high level summary of findings.

Since not all projects are the same, the assessment approach should not be the same for all projects. The key is for the assessment team to understand stakeholders, the corporation culture and the project culture, and customize the approach to align with their expectations and styles, while still meeting the stated objectives.

Packaging and presenting are important

All of the planning, assessing and recommendations come together in the final report, and so the report should be well organized and convey the key messages in a way that they are well structured, fact based, and perceived as fair and credible. Careful thought should be taken to recognize the audience of the report, and to ensure that it aligns with their expectations and style. Lastly, the facilitator should recognize the response of the audience during the presentation and modify accordingly.

7.2 Checklists

This section is meant to be a reference for the content within the book, organized into checklists which include the IT roles, questions to ask during the interviews, organized by role and focus area for document reviews.

7.2.1 IT roles

Table 7.1 lists out the typical roles on an IT project which may be relevant to be interviewed during the project assessment. While this is not every possible role, it does represent the major functions and roles within a project. Each role has a specific focus and set of responsibilities within the project which should be considered during the interviewing process. Some of these focus areas are noted below.

Table 7.1: Typical roles on an IT project

Role	Description and Focus
Sponsor	The overall sponsor of the project, who is the champion for the outcomes of the project
IT Lead	The overall lead for the technology work, ultimately accountable for the delivery of the project
Business Lead	The overall lead for the business work, ultimately accountable for the delivery of the project
Project Manager	The person managing the project and accountable for the creation, monitoring and execution of the plan, and activities within the plan
Project Management Office (PMO)	The team of people who manage project operational functions, such as financials, resources, vendor contracts, and documents. In some projects, the project manager performs these functions without a separate team
Business Analyst	The team member who is accountable for facilitating requirements from business experts and documenting them as system specifications
Subject Matter Expert	The person who is an expert in a specific business area and who provides input into requirements
Architect/Designer	The person who designs the technology solution required to meet the business requirements
Developer	The person who develops the technology solution and fixes any defects found during testing
Infrastructure Engineer	The person who designs and develops the infrastructure solution required to meet business requirements
Test Planner	The person who defines the test cases and conditions to ensure that the solution meets the business requirements
Tester	The person who executes the test conditions and logs any defects. Note that there are several types of testers (e.g. system, user, performance, etc.)
Operational Readiness	The person who plans to make sure that the organization, processes, and tools are prepared for when the technology solution gets delivered
Business Process Designer	The person who designs the business process which accompanies the technology solution
Vendors	Vendors may perform key roles on the project, supplement key resources, or provide a specific skill to the team

7.2.2 Project interviews

Chapter 4 organizes the collection of information by functional area, but the interviews occur with specific roles. This section organizes the focus areas and considerations by role and breaks them out by function. This will allow for interviews to be efficient with time and focus on several areas during one session.

Table 7.2: Interview roles: Sponsor

Function	Focus and Considerations
Schedule Management	• Confirm proper communication of milestones, critical path, and progress against schedule commitments
Communications Management	• Obtain their views on the adequacy of project communications • Confirm that they are getting what they need, with the right level of information

Table 7.3: Interview roles: IT Lead

Function	Focus and Considerations
Structure and Governance	• Discuss perspectives on how the project is structured and governed • Discuss alignment of business and IT and any concerns or gaps
Schedule Management	• Confirm proper communication of milestones, critical path, and progress against schedule commitments
Cost Management	• Get perspectives on how well project financials and estimates are managed • Confirm they are getting the right level of transparency into project financials and financial health
Resource Management	• Get perspectives on any resource challenges on the project
Communications Management	• Obtain their views on the adequacy of project communications – are they getting what they need, with the right level of information?

RAID Management	• Discuss how they feel about risk, issue and decision management, and confirm that they have enough transparency into risks and issues • Discuss if they feel that issues and risks get escalated to them in a timely manner
Vendor Management	• Understand the strategy for the project around using vendors and in what expected capacities

Table 7.4: Interview roles: Business Lead

Function	Focus and Considerations
Structure and Governance	• Discuss perspectives on how the project is structured and being governed • Discuss alignment of business and IT, and any concerns or gaps
Scope and Change Management	• Confirm that there is clarity of project scope for the project and no open clarifications required • Discuss their view of the scope and change management process
Cost Management	• Get perspectives on how well project financials and estimates are managed • Confirm they are getting the right level of transparency into project financials and financial health
Resource Management	• Get perspectives on any resource challenges on the project
Communications Management	• Obtain their views on the adequacy of project communications – are they getting what they need, with the right level of information?
RAID Management	• Discuss how they feel about risk, issue and decision management, and confirm that they have enough transparency into risks and issues • Discuss if they feel that issues and risks get escalated to them in a timely manner

Table 7.5: Interview roles: Project Manager

Function	Focus and Considerations
Structure and Governance	• Discuss how the project is structured • Discuss alignment of business and IT roles, and any concerns or gaps • Discuss how the business case, objectives and goals are being communicated, and managed, within the project • Discuss how well the project is following the documented approach within the charter, business case, and project management approach
Scope and Change Management	• Discuss how scope is managed and documented on the project • Discuss the approach for reviews and sign offs of requirements • Assess if the change control approach is documented and understood
Schedule Management	• Discuss how the schedule was created with activities, durations and milestones • Confirm that there is a formal project plan with activities, dates, names, and durations • Discuss how the plan is tracked and updated on a regular basis • Discuss what techniques are used to monitor and report on plan progress (e.g. earned value, percent complete, etc.) • Discuss how the project is tracking to its schedule commitments • Discuss how changes and issues get modelled to understand impacts on milestones
Cost Management	• Discuss how the project estimates were developed • Discuss how project financials are managed including forecasting for all of the cost types, capturing and tracking actual costs, conducting variance analysis, and reporting • Discuss how cost is managed in the change control process

	• Review how the project is tracking against the budget
Resource Management	• Review the project organizational structure and associated roles and responsibilities • Identify any unfilled project roles • Discuss if there are any challenges with resource competencies or allocations to not be able to perform their work • Discuss the morale of the team to understand challenges • Understand what they are spending their time on
Communications Management	• Review the communications plan and stakeholder matrix • Review the process for developing status reports including what information is used, the sources of that information, and how the reports get presented
RAID Management	• Review how they use the RAID tools to manage the program • Discuss how risks and issues get escalated and any challenges they have • Discuss how decisions get made and any challenges they have
Vendor Management	• Understand how the project uses vendors and in what capacities • Discuss how the vendor relationship is managed • Discuss how the contract was set up including quality reviews and performance metrics • Discuss how well the partnerships are working with the vendors
SDLC Management	• Understand their perspectives on where there may be resource or delivery risks with respect to the SDLC activities

Table 7.6: Interview roles: PMO

Function	Focus and Considerations
Structure and Governance	• Get perspectives on how the project is structured and governed • Get their perspectives on the clarity of business case, objectives, and priorities and alignment to their work
Scope and Change Management	• Discuss how scope is managed and documented on the project • Discuss the approach for reviews and sign offs of requirements • Assess if the change control approach is documented and understood
Schedule Management	• Discuss the approach for schedule creation, management, and tracking • Discuss alignment of change management and schedule management
Cost Management	• Discuss the approach for developing project estimates including involvement of the team • Discuss the approach for managing financials including forecasting for all of the cost types, capturing and tracking actual costs, conducting variance analysis, and reporting • Discuss the approach for cost management in the change control process • Discuss the approach for management reporting including variance explanations and approvals for cost overruns
Resource Management	• Discuss the approach for resource management on the project including planning of resources, capacity planning, alignment to work, and forecasting of resource needs • Review the process for defining roles and responsibilities • Review the onboarding process for new resources

Communications Management	• Discuss the approach for managing project communications including identification of stakeholders, communication mechanisms, and plans • Understand the approach for maintaining, versioning, storing, and approving key documents
RAID Management	• Review the approach for risk, issue, action item, and decision management
Vendor Management	• Discuss the approach for managing vendors, contracts, and invoices
SDLC Management	• Review the key SDLC process, gates, and approach for the project

Table 7.7: Interview roles: Business Analyst

Function	Focus and Considerations
Structure and Governance	• Get perspectives on how the project is structured and governed • Get their perspectives on the clarity of business case, objectives, and priorities and alignment to their work
Scope and Change Management	• Discuss how scope is documented and managed including templates, tools used, and reporting • Confirm that the right business experts are available and aligned to the project • Confirm that the review and approval process is adequate including the identification of key business resources to perform these
Schedule Management	• Discuss the approach for schedule creation, management, and tracking • Ask if they are aware of the key milestones of the plan
Cost Management	• Discuss the involvement of the team in the estimates and management of financials
Resource Management	• Discuss if resources have what they need to complete activities

	• Confirm if roles and responsibilities are clear • Discuss the morale of the team to understand challenges
Communications Management	• Confirm that the team members feel like they are getting relevant project information in a timely manner
RAID Management	• Determine if they feel that risks and issues get escalated properly and addressed quickly • Discuss how they feel about decisions being made in a timely manner • Discuss how they feel about action items being tracked
Vendor Management	• Discuss how well vendors are being used on the project and any challenges that the team is having with them
SDLC Management	• Review the approach for facilitating and documenting requirements • Discuss their perspectives on the risks, or challenges, with collecting requirements

Table 7.8: Interview roles: Subject Matter Expert

Function	Focus and Considerations
Scope and Change Management	• Confirm how the subject matter experts are leveraged to facilitate requirements, and get their perspectives on how well this is managed • Get their perspective on scope reviews and sign offs
SDLC Management	• Discuss their perspectives on the risks, or challenges, with documenting requirements

Table 7.9: Interview roles: Architect/Designer

Function	Focus and Considerations
Structure and Governance	• Get perspectives on how the project is structured and governed • Get their perspectives on the clarity of business case, objectives, and priorities and alignment to their work

Schedule Management	• Discuss the approach for schedule creation, management, and tracking • Ask if they are aware of the key milestones of the plan
Cost Management	• Discuss involvement of the team in the estimates and management of financials
Resource Management	• Discuss if resources have what they need to complete activities • Confirm if roles and responsibilities are clear • Discuss the morale of the team to understand challenges
Communications Management	• Confirm that the team members feel like they are getting relevant project information in a timely manner
RAID Management	• Determine if they feel that risks and issues get escalated properly and addressed quickly • Discuss how they feel about decisions being made in a timely manner • Discuss how they feel about action items being tracked
Vendor Management	• Discuss how well vendors are being used on the project and any challenges that the team is having with them
SDLC Management	• Review the approach for translating the requirements into designs and system specifications • Discuss their perspectives on the risks, or challenges, with designing the system solutions • Discuss the approach for the solution including integration points, maintainability, scalability, and performance

Table 7.10: Interview roles: Developer

Function	Focus and Considerations
Structure and Governance	• Get their perspectives on how the project is structured and governed

	• Get their perspectives on the clarity of business case, objectives, and priorities and alignment to their work
Schedule Management	• Discuss the approach for schedule creation, management, and tracking • Ask if they are aware of the key milestones of the plan
Cost Management	• Discuss the involvement of the team in the estimates and management of financials
Resource Management	• Discuss if resources have what they need to complete activities • Confirm if roles and responsibilities are clear • Discuss the morale of the team to understand challenges
Communications Management	• Confirm that the team members feel like they are getting relevant project information in a timely manner
RAID Management	• Determine if they feel that risks and issues get escalated properly and addressed quickly • Discuss how they feel about decisions being made in a timely manner • Discuss how they feel about action items being tracked
Vendor Management	• Discuss how well vendors are being used on the project and any challenges that the team is having with them
SDLC Management	• Discuss their perspectives on the risks, or challenges, with developing code

Table 7.11: Interview roles: Test Planner and Tester

Function	Focus and Considerations
Structure and Governance	• Get their perspectives on how the project is structured and governed • Get their perspectives on the clarity of business case, objectives, and priorities and alignment to their work
Schedule Management	• Discuss the approach for schedule creation, management, and tracking

	• Ask if they are aware of the key milestones of the plan
Cost Management	• Discuss the involvement of the team in the estimates and management of financials
Resource Management	• Discuss if resources have what they need to complete activities • Confirm if roles and responsibilities are clear • Discuss the morale of the team to understand challenges
Communications Management	• Confirm that the team members feel like they are getting relevant project information in a timely manner
RAID Management	• Determine if they feel that risks and issues get escalated properly and addressed quickly • Discuss how they feel about decisions being made in a timely manner • Discuss how they feel about action items being tracked
Vendor Management	• Discuss how well vendors are being used on the project and any challenges that the team is having with them
SDLC Management	• Review the approach for the test strategy or plans • Discuss their perspectives on the risks, or challenges, with test planning • Discuss their perspectives on the risks, or challenges, with test execution

Table 7.12: Interview roles: Operational Readiness

Function	Focus and Considerations
Structure and Governance	• Get their perspectives on how the project is structured and governed • Get their perspectives on the clarity of business case, objectives, and priorities and alignment to their work
Schedule Management	• Discuss the approach for schedule creation, management, and tracking • Ask if they are aware of the key milestones of the plan

Cost Management	• Discuss the involvement of the team in the estimates and management of financials
Resource Management	• Discuss if resources have what they need to complete activities • Confirm if roles and responsibilities are clear • Discuss the morale of the team to understand challenges
Communications Management	• Confirm that the team members feel like they are getting relevant project information in a timely manner
RAID Management	• Determine if they feel that risks and issues get escalated properly and addressed quickly • Discuss how they feel about decisions being made in a timely manner • Discuss how they feel about action items being tracked
Vendor Management	• Discuss how well vendors are being used on the project and any challenges that the team is having with them
SDLC Management	• Discuss the approach for preparing the organization for the deployment of the project scope including contingency planning, release planning, training, and any warranty support or command center strategies • Discuss the approach for updating operational support processes, such as incident management, change management, and help desk procedures • Review the key deployment risks for the project

Table 7.13: Interview roles: Vendors

Function	Focus and Considerations
Vendor Management	• If there are strategic vendors, or vendors in certain roles on the project, they should be considered for interviews, to get their perspectives on the project and its risks

	• They should be asked the questions for their respective roles on the project
SDLC Management	• Discuss any challenges, or risks, that the vendors observe

7.2.3 Project documents

This section provides an inventory of typical IT project documents which should be considered for the assessment, as well as some possible focus areas for that document during the project assessment.

Table 7.14: Documents: Project structure and governance

Document	Focus and Considerations
Business Case	• Business problem has been identified • Business benefits are identified • Business case has been approved and signed off
Project Charter	• Project objectives are documented • Project structure is documented • Includes clarity of IT and business roles and responsibilities • Charter has been approved and signed off
Project Management Approach	• Documented approach for managing the project including management of finances, resources, schedule, issues, risks, actions, and other operational items • Document the delivery methodology that will be used
Governance Approach	• Approach for how the project will be governed is documented (e.g. steering committees, approvals, phase gates, sign offs, reviews, etc.)

Table 7.15: Documents: Scope and change management

Document	Focus and Considerations
Scope Management Approach	• Documented approach for managing, tracking, and signing off on scope

Centralized Scope	• Scope documented in one place and maintained in a repository • Approval of scope documented
Change Management Approach	• Documented approach for identifying, assessing, estimating, and deciding on changes • Approach for obtaining approval • Approach for updating documents once change is approved
Change Log	• Formalized change log which captures key information (change, impact, disposition, etc.)

Table 7.16: Documents: Schedule management

Document	Focus and Considerations
Approach	• Approach for developing and managing plans and dependencies • Approach for tracking and reporting on progress and schedule risks • Document how to assess schedule impacts of risks, issues, and changes • For programs, document how to manage the schedule across projects, manage dependencies, and roll up progress
Project Plan	• Uses corporation standard tool and includes corporation standard SDLC activities • Documented schedule with key activities, milestones, and durations • People assigned to activities • Identify and document dependencies between activities • Identification of a critical path • Properly maintained, tracked, and reported • Review the plans to understand progress against scheduled commitments
Dependencies	• Dependencies are identified and tracked (within project, across projects and external to the project or program)
Tracking	• Approach for tracking work completed and progress towards milestones

	• Approach for identifying at-risk activities and action plans • Plans are maintained (e.g. milestones past due date are either marked as complete or reforecast to new dates)

Table 7.17: Documents: Cost management

Document	Focus and Considerations
Financial Management Approach	• Approach for managing financials including estimation, forecasting, tracking actuals, variance reporting, and management reporting • Documented calendar of financial processes and timings • Alignment of project cost management approach with corporation standard approach, tools, and process • Alignment to change management process to assess impact of proposed changes on project cost
Estimation	• Documented approach and tools for estimating project components and developing the project forecast • Approach to maintain estimation tools based on historical financial costs
Cost Tracking	• Tracking of actual costs as they get incurred • Reporting of actual cost against budget • Alignment to corporation standards • Review financial reports and variances to get a sense of how the project is tracking against budget goals
Reporting	• Consistent and accurate reporting of financial costs and variances to key stakeholders

Table 7.18: Documents: Resource management

Document	Focus and Considerations
Resource Management Approach	• Approach for managing resources including planning for capacity, tracking resources, and onboarding

Organization Chart	• Review to see if a structure exists which includes the key roles and current content • Names should be assigned to the primary roles
Roles and Responsibilities	• Roles and responsibility matrix which aligns project roles to the organization chart and deliverables (also known as a RACI matrix) • Confirm that roles and responsibilities are documented and align with corporation standard definitions
Resource Roster	• Identification of the team members with their corresponding roles on the project and organization • Confirm alignment of resources to work with allocations by month • Confirm start and end dates for resources
Onboarding plan	• Confirm onboarding approach exists and the content is current
Training	• Training plan for specific skills and needs

Table 7.19: Documents: Communications and stakeholder management

Document	Focus and Considerations
Stakeholder Matrix	• Identification of all project stakeholders • Understanding of what information each stakeholder needs
Communication Approach and Plan	• Documented plan for communications to different stakeholders • Plan for different types of communication formats and frequencies to various audiences (e.g. weekly status report) • Plan for communicating team changes or project announcements • Approach for management of documents including folder structure and versions
Project Document Inventory	• Central location for storing project documents • Structure of repository is logical and organized • Version controls for key documents

Sample Status Report and Management Report	• Demonstrates progress updates against milestones and commitments • Transparency in risks and issues for management attention • Determine if status is driven from metrics and facts
Sample Meeting Agendas and Minutes	• Structured agendas and meeting minute templates

Table 7.20: Documents: RAID management

Document	Focus and Considerations
Risk Management Approach	• Documented approach including identification of risks, weighting of risks, and assigning actions
Issue Management Approach	• Documented approach for issue identification, escalation, and resolution
Action Item Management Approach	• Documented approach for identifying, tracking, and following up on project action items
Decision Management Approach	• Documented approach for making project decisions and tracking decision information
Risk Log	• Risks are managed and tracked in a central risk log • Confirm that actions are identified with owners and dates for each risk • The risk log is properly maintained without many open items past due dates
Issue Log	• Issues are managed and tracked in a central issue log • Confirm that actions are identified with owners and dates for each issue • The issue log is properly maintained without many open items past due dates
Action Item Log	• Actions are managed and tracked in a central action item log • Confirm that actions are identified with owners and dates for each issue

	• The action item log is properly maintained without many open items past due dates
Decision Log	• Decisions tracked in a central location which includes information on the decision, who made it, and when it was made

Table 7.21: Documents: Vendor management

Document	Focus and Considerations
Vendor Management Approach	• Approach for vendors documented including when to use vendors, approach for procuring vendors, and tracking methods • Approach for managing the contracts, invoices, and finances of vendors • Approach for reporting on vendor resources, spend, progress, and risks
Vendor Inventory	• Inventory of all vendors working on the project
Vendor Document Repository	• Review the location for vendor contracts and invoices
Vendor Scorecard	• Some corporations require vendor scorecards so the assessment may want to review these for insights into the vendor relationship

Table 7.22: Documents: SDLC management

Document	Focus and Considerations
SDLC	• Standard methodology documented and being used on the project • Roles and responsibilities should be documented for SDLC artifacts
Requirements	• Requirements management including the collection of requirements, what tools to use, the sign off process, and traceability • Documented business and functional requirements which may include process flows, data, and other technical requirements (e.g. performance and security) • Requirement documents should have reviews and sign offs

Design	• Approach for documenting designs, confirming that designs meet requirements, and sign offs • Review the design documents to see how the approach was used • Documented approach for nonfunctional requirements, such as scalability, maintainability, security, and performance
Build	• Code delivery • Confirm that unit test results are documented and demonstrate ample testing
Test	• Test approach and strategy document a comprehensive approach for all types of testing including data, environments, tools, the defect management process, and metrics for reporting • Test plans should follow the test strategy and approach • Test results confirm that testing was completed per the plan • Reports and metrics should exist for transparency of testing progress
Operational Readiness	• Approach for operational readiness which includes planning for releases, contingency planning, training, and organizational readiness • Documented changes to operational processes, such as incident management, change management, and service management • Documented release and contingency plans for project releases • Project closure documents to track lessons learned

7.3 Additional references

This book has covered many topics broadly and so this final section provides some references in each of the functional areas, should the reader be interested in additional information and best practices. These are captured in Table 7.23. There are many other materials in the marketplace but these are ones that I have found helpful for reference in my career and profession.

Table 7.23: Additional references

Function	References
Project Assessments	• <u>Book</u>: *Global Technology Audit Guide 12: Auditing IT Projects* (The Institute of Internal Auditors) – comprehensive reference for IT audits • <u>Website</u>: *www.theiia.org* – the Institute of Internal Auditors website which provides standards and guides and certifications • <u>Website</u>: *www.isaca.org* – the Information Systems Audit and Control Association website which houses best practices on information systems • <u>Website</u>: *www.knowledgeleader.com* – provides tools and best practices for project audits
Structure and Governance	• <u>Book</u>: *Applying Guiding Principles of Effective Program Delivery* (Kerry Wills) – describes how to structure and run IT programs • <u>Book</u>: *The Standard for Program Management* (PMI) which outlines program management scope, lifecycle and processes • <u>Book</u>: *Project Management Body of Knowledge* (PMI) – initial chapters focus on developing a charter and identifying stakeholders
Scope and Change Management	• <u>Website</u>: *www.iiba.org* – International Institute of Business Analysts website which provides resources and certifications on requirements gathering and scope management • <u>Book</u>: *Project Management Body of Knowledge* (PMI) – contains several chapters on identifying scope, change control and project controls
Schedule Management	• <u>Book</u>: *Practice Standard for Work Breakdown Structures* (PMI) – good foundation for building a WBS

	• <u>Book</u>: *Practice Standard for Scheduling* (PMI) – reviews development and management of schedules • <u>Book</u>: *Project Management Body of Knowledge* (PMI) – contains several chapters on managing activities and creating a WBS
Cost Management	• <u>Book</u>: *The Practice Standard for Project Estimation* (PMI) – reviews various methods and best practices for estimation • <u>Book</u>: *Project Management Body of Knowledge* (PMI) – has several chapters on estimation, cost management and budgeting
Resource Management	• <u>Book</u>: *Project Management Body of Knowledge* (PMI) – reviews human resource management principles
Communications Management	• <u>Book</u>: *Project Management Body of Knowledge* (PMI) – contains several chapters on communications planning and management
RAID Management	• <u>Book</u>: *Practice Standard for Project Risk Management* (PMI) – industry standard on risk management • <u>Book</u>: *Project Management Body of Knowledge* (PMI) – contains several chapters on risk management
Vendor Management	• <u>Book</u>: *Project Management Body of Knowledge* (PMI) – contains several chapters on procurement management
SDLC Management	• <u>Website</u>: *http://en.wikipedia.org/wiki/Systems_development_life_cycle* –Wikipedia site that contains an overview of the IT SDLC, along with several other references and books

REFERENCES

Camp, Robert C. 1989. *Benchmarking: The Search for Industry Best Practices that Lead to Superior Performance.* ASQC Quality Press. Milwaukee, Wisconsin

Forrester Research. 2014. Global Tech Market Outlook 2013 To 2014

Hubbard, Douglas. 2009. *The Failure of Risk Management: Why It's Broken and How to Fix It.* John Wiley & Sons

Keshishian, Mariette and Walkow, Patricia. 2010. *Where People and Projects Meet: Tools and techniques for understanding and managing the people side of projects.* CreateSpace Independent Publishing Platform

Project Management Institute. 2010. The Practice Standard for Project Estimation

Project Management Institute. 2013. The Standard for Program Management Third Edition

The Institute of Internal Auditors. 2009. Global Technology Audit Guide 12: Auditing IT Projects

The Standish Group International. 2014. CHAOS Report

Wills, Kerry R. 2013, *Applying Guiding Principles of Effective Program Delivery.* Taylor & Francis. Boca Raton, Florida

ITG RESOURCES

IT Governance Ltd sources, creates and delivers products and services to meet the real-world, evolving IT governance needs of today's organisations, directors, managers and practitioners.

The ITG website (*www.itgovernance.co.uk*) is the international one-stop-shop for corporate and IT governance information, advice, guidance, books, tools, training and consultancy.

Publishing Services

IT Governance Publishing (ITGP) is the world's leading IT-GRC publishing imprint that is wholly owned by IT Governance Ltd.

With books and tools covering all IT governance, risk and compliance frameworks, we are the publisher of choice for authors and distributors alike, producing unique and practical publications of the highest quality, in the latest formats available, which readers will find invaluable.

www.itgovernancepublishing.co.uk is the website dedicated to ITGP. Other titles published by ITGP that may be of interest include:

- Swanson on Internal Auditing

  www.itgovernance.co.uk/shop/p-1142-swanson-on-internal-auditing-raising-the-bar.aspx

- Agile Governance and Audit

  www.itgovernance.co.uk/shop/p-1616-agile-governance-and-audit.aspx

- 50 Top IT Project Management Challenges
www.itgovernance.co.uk/shop/p-325-50-top-it-project-
management-challenges.aspx.

We also offer a range of off-the-shelf toolkits that give comprehensive, customisable documents to help users create the specific documentation they need to properly implement a management system or standard. Written by experienced practitioners and based on the latest best practice, ITGP toolkits can save months of work for organisations working towards compliance with a given standard.

To see the full range of toolkits available please see:

www.itgovernance.co.uk/shop/c-129-toolkits.aspx.

Books and tools published by IT Governance Publishing (ITGP) are available from all business booksellers and the following websites:

www.itgovernance.eu   *www.itgovernanceusa.com*
www.itgovernance.in   *www.itgovernancesa.co.za*
www.itgovernance.asia

Training Services

If you're managing a project in your organisation, you may be interested in IT Governance's range of project management training courses, accredited by the PMI® (Project Management Institute).

The PMI's CAPM® (Certified Associate in Project Management) and PMP® (Project Management Professional) qualifications are globally recognised, and highly sought-after by professional project managers throughout the world.

CAPM

The entry-level CAPM qualification is aimed at relatively new project managers and others involved in project management who seek professional accreditation or an initial understanding of the PMBOK® Guide approach to project management. Delegates should check their eligibility on the PMI website (*www.pmi.org/Certification/Certified-Associate-in-Project-Management-CAPM.aspx*) before booking their course places. IT Governance holds two CAPM courses:

- **CAPM Certification Exam Preparation Workshop**
  www.itgovernance.co.uk/shop/p-419-capm-certification-exam-preparation-workshop-training-course.aspx.
- **Preparing for the CAPM Exam Training Course**
  www.itgovernance.co.uk/shop/p-1040-preparing-for-the-capm-exam-training-course.aspx.

PMP

Aimed at more experienced project managers, the PMP qualification is recognised globally as an indication that holders have the experience, education and competency to lead and direct projects. Delegates should check their eligibility on the PMI website (*www.pmi.org/Certification/Project-Management-Professional-PMP.aspx*) before booking their course places. IT Governance holds two PMP courses:

- **Preparing for the PMP Exam Training Course**
  www.itgovernance.co.uk/shop/p-1041-preparing-for-the-pmp-exam-training-course.aspx.

- **The Complete PMP Training Course**
  www.itgovernance.co.uk/shop/p-1164-the-complete-pmp-project-management-professional-training-course.aspx.

  For more information on all of IT Governance's PMBOK training courses, visit *www.itgovernance.co.uk/pmbok-course.aspx.*

Professional Services and Consultancy

At IT Governance we recognise the importance of delivering services that are business-led, rather than shaped by technology. Whether you need an extra pair of hands or in-depth project support during the implementation phase, we can help you to ensure a 100% successful outcome.

If you're conducting an *ITIL* adoption or *ISO/IEC 20000* implementation project, the IT Governance professional services team can tailor a package of consultancy, training and project resources to meet all your requirements.

With a clear focus on developing your knowledge, skills and confidence through our value-for-money approach, we will enable every member of your staff to take ownership of the improvement process and deliver consistently high-quality, efficient and effective IT services.

Our consultants will help you design IT services that will have the correct utility and warranty for your organisation and users. Having worked with many organisations during this stage of other ITSM, ITIL and ISO20000 projects, we understand the common issues and will help you to overcome them.

For more information on our ITSM, ITIL and ISO20000 consultancy, please visit *www.itgovernance.co.uk/itsm-itil-iso20000-consultancy.aspx*.

For general information on our other consultancy services, including for ISO27001, ISO22301, Cyber Essentials, the PCI DSS, Data Protection and more, please visit *www.itgovernance.co.uk/consulting.aspx*.

Newsletter

IT governance is one of the hottest topics in business today, not least because it is also the fastest moving.

You can stay up to date with the latest developments across the whole spectrum of IT governance subject matter, including; risk management, information security, ITIL and IT service management, project governance, compliance and so much more, by subscribing to ITG's core publications and topic alert emails.

Simply visit our subscription centre and select your preferences:

www.itgovernance.co.uk/newsletter.aspx.

Lightning Source UK Ltd.
Milton Keynes UK
UKOW06f2223220515

252057UK00001B/17/P

9 781849 287364